W9-ABX-226

THE FEMINIST
MOVEMENT

AMERICAN
SOCIAL
MOVEMENTS

THE FEMINIST MOVEMENT

Nick Treanor, *Book Editor*

Daniel Leone, *President*
Bonnie Szumski, *Publisher*
Scott Barbour, *Managing Editor*

GREENHAVEN PRESS
SAN DIEGO, CALIFORNIA

THOMSON
™
GALE

Detroit • New York • San Diego • San Francisco
Boston • New Haven, Conn. • Waterville, Maine
London • Munich

Every effort has been made to trace the owners of copyrighted material. The articles in this volume may have been edited for content, length, and/or reading level. The titles have been changed to enhance the editorial purpose.

Library of Congress Cataloging-in-Publication Data

The feminist movement / Nick Treanor, book editor.
  p. cm. — (American social movements series)
  Includes bibliographical references and index.
  Summary: Discusses the development of the feminist movement, including world involvement and personal stories
    ISBN 0-7377-1050-0 (lib. : alk. paper) —
ISBN 0-7377-1049-7 (pbk. : alk. paper)
   1. Feminism—United States. 2. Women—United States—Social conditions. [1. Feminism. 2. Women.] I. Title.
II. American social movements.

HQ1426 .T775 2002
305.42'0973—dc21   2001007289

Cover photo: © Ricardo Watson/Archive Photos
Library of Congress, 22, 98, 166, 193

Cover caption: Feminists Bella Abzug, Gloria Steinem, Dick Gregory, and Betty Friedan in ERA march, Washington, D.C.

Copyright © 2002 by Greenhaven Press,
an imprint of The Gale Group
10911 Technology Place, San Diego, CA 92127

Printed in the USA

CONTENTS

ment and its heroes are largely ignored in most history books.

Chapter 2 • THE PERSONAL IS POLITICAL: FEMINISM'S SECOND WAVE

women, and many traditional feminist issues are being neglected. Feminism should return to its egalitarian roots.

Chapter 4 • FEMINIST FRONTIERS: AMERICAN WOMEN AND THE WORLD

Chapter 5 • PERSONAL NARRATIVES: VOICES FROM THE VANGUARD

feminism could never completely fill that need, it
gave the strength to face the hard truths of the world.

When a woman notices that she is oppressed, it is
easy to think that this must mean that men are bad
and willing oppressors. But she may come to notice
that she herself has benefited from injustices, particularly from race or class injustices, without being
aware of them. This can lead her to re-think her
attitudes toward men.

Society demands that people dress in such a way that
everyone can instantly tell whether they are men or
women. People who dress androgynously are reject-
ing a system in which people are judged based on
their gender.

FOREWORD

H istorians Gary T. Marx and Douglas McAdam define a
social movement as "organized efforts to promote or resist change in society that rely, at least in part, on noninstitu-
tionalized forms of political action." Examining American social movements broadens and vitalizes the study of history by
allowing students to observe the efforts of ordinary individuals and groups to oppose the established values of their era, often in unconventional ways. The civil rights movement of the
twentieth century, for example, began as an effort to challenge
legalized racial segregation and garner social and political rights
for African Americans. Several grassroots organizations—
groups of ordinary citizens committed to social activism—
came together to organize boycotts, sit-ins, voter registration
drives, and demonstrations to counteract racial discrimination.
Initially, the movement faced massive opposition from white
citizens, who had long been accustomed to the social standards
that required the separation of the races in almost all areas of
life. But the movement's consistent use of an innovative form
of protest—nonviolent direct action—eventually aroused the
public conscience, which in turn paved the way for major legislative victories such as the Civil Rights Act of 1964 and the
Voting Rights Act of 1965. Examining the civil rights movement reveals how ordinary people can use nonstandard political strategies to change society.

Investigating the style, tactics, personalities, and ideologies
of American social movements also encourages students to
learn about aspects of history and culture that may receive
scant attention in textbooks. As scholar Eric Foner notes,
American history "has been constructed not only in congressional debates and political treatises, but also on plantations and
picket lines, in parlors and bedrooms. Frederick Douglass, Eu-
gene V. Debs, and Margaret Sanger . . . are its architects as well
as Thomas Jefferson and Abraham Lincoln." While not all

American social movements garner popular support or lead to epoch-changing legislation, they each offer their own unique insight into a young democracy's political dialogue.

Each book in Greenhaven's American Social Movements series allows readers to follow the general progression of a particular social movement—examining its historical roots and beginnings in earlier chapters and relatively recent and contemporary information (or even the movement's demise) in later chapters. With the incorporation of both primary and secondary sources, as well as writings by both supporters and critics of the movement, each anthology provides an engaging panoramic view of its subject. Selections include a variety of readings, such as book excerpts, newspaper articles, speeches, manifestos, literary essays, interviews, and personal narratives. The editors of each volume aim to include the voices of movement leaders and participants as well as the opinions of historians, social analysts, and individuals who have been affected by the movement. This comprehensive approach gives students the opportunity to view these movements both as participants have experienced them and as historians and critics have interpreted them.

Every volume in the American Social Movements series includes an introductory essay that presents a broad historical overview of the movement in question. The annotated table of contents and comprehensive index help readers quickly locate material of interest. Each selection is preceded by an introductory paragraph that summarizes the article's content and provides historical context when necessary. Several other research aids are also present, including brief excerpts of supplementary material, a chronology of major events pertaining to the movement, and an accessible bibliography.

The Greenhaven Press American Social Movements series offers readers an informative introduction to some of the most fascinating groups and ideas in American history. The contents of each anthology provide a valuable resource for general readers as well as for enthusiasts of American political science, history, and culture.

Feminism in America

The Boston Tea Party, as most schoolchildren in America know, marked the early stirrings of the American Revolution. On a cold December night in 1773, a group of colonists protesting British rule crept aboard tea ships moored in Boston Harbor and tossed 342 crates of tea into the sea. King George III was not amused, but the American colonists, moved by the political ideals of liberty and democracy, had not been afraid of upsetting him. Indeed, just three years later Thomas Jefferson would pen the Declaration of Independence, formally setting in motion the American Revolution, by which the colonists threw off English rule.

Although most schoolchildren are familiar with the Boston Tea Party, fewer have heard about another tea party, this one a little more traditional but no less revolutionary, which took place in upstate New York on July 13, 1848. At the home of Jane and Richard Hunt, wealthy Quakers living in Waterloo, New York, five female friends sat down for an afternoon of tea and conversation. In addition to Hunt, in attendance were Elizabeth Cady Stanton, Mary Ann McClintock, Lucretia Mott, and her sister, Martha Coffin Wright. Although none knew it at the time, it would prove to be a historic occasion.

In time the conversation on that July afternoon turned to the situation of women in the republic, and the women let their grievances be known. The American Revolution had been fought on the principles of liberty and democracy, but in 1848 the republic, in its seventieth year of existence, was still a long way from ensuring liberty and justice for all. Just as American colonists seventy years earlier had resented being ruled by a foreign king, the women gathered there considered themselves subject to injustice at the hands of a government in which they had no say. Indeed, the colonists' famous rallying cry "No taxation without representation" could well have issued from the women gathered at the tea party, who, like all American women, were forbidden from voting. The concerns voiced that afternoon were not limited to women's inability to vote, however. Among other things, in 1848 married women in most states could not own property or control their own money, husbands had considerable legal power over their wives, divorce and custody laws favored men, and most occupations, especially well-rewarded ones, and almost all universities and colleges were closed to women. It was not the first time women in America had discussed this theme. This group, however, decided to do something about it.

A HISTORIC CONVENTION

Within two days, a small advertisement appeared in the *Seneca County Courier*, drawing attention to "a convention to discuss the social, civil and religious condition and the rights of women." The two-day meeting opened on July 19, 1848—just six days after the tea party—at the Wesleyan Chapel in Seneca Falls. Although the meeting marked a historic turn for women in America and is often taken as the founding moment in the American women's movement, it had been centuries in the making. The social and political situation that sparked the 1848 convention was nothing new, nor was it limited to the American republic. Early Roman law, for instance, had described women as children and consequently afforded them fewer rights and protections. Although the European cultures from which white Americans descended were not without prominent and powerful women—Queen Elizabeth of England and Catherine the Great of Russia are notable examples—much of European and American society viewed women as naturally inferior to men in intellectual and political spheres. Indeed, during the thirteenth century, Thomas Aquinas, one of the most eminent Christian theologians, had said that women's "unique role is in conception . . . since for other purposes men would be better assisted by other men." It is hard to say whether those in attendance at that first women's rights convention knew the long history that preceded the social conditions of life in America in 1848. What is clear, however, is that they found those conditions unjust and were determined to change them.

Just as Thomas Jefferson had listed American complaints against the British king in the Declaration of Independence, the women and men gathered in Wesleyan Chapel discussed and endorsed the Declaration of Sentiments and Resolutions. This document, written largely by Stanton and deliberately echoing Jefferson's treatise, outlines the grievances those gathered felt toward the prevailing legal and social arrangement concerning women. All but one of the resolutions were debated and discussed and, with a few amendments, unanimously endorsed. The controversial resolution called for extending the franchise to women, a proposal that was shocking to many gathered there, as progressively minded as they were. The discussion over whether to include a demand for women's suffrage was intense. Even Stanton, who was noted for her powerful oratory skills, was unable to convince a majority to endorse the resolution. At last Frederick Douglass, a black abolitionist and a noted orator himself, rose to speak. "Suffrage is the power to choose rulers and make laws," he reminded the assembly, "and the right by which all others are secured." The resolution passed, but barely.

As exciting and promising as that two-day convention was for those in attendance, few harbored illusions about the road ahead:

> In entering upon the great work before us, we anticipate no small amount of misconception, misrepresentation and ridicule, but we shall use every instrumentality within our power to effect our object. We shall employ agents, circulate tracts, petition the state and national legislatures, and endeavor to enlist the pulpit and the press in our behalf. We hope this convention will be followed by a series of conventions, embracing every part of the country.

So ends the Declaration of Sentiments. The women's movement in America had begun.

THE LONG ROAD TO SUFFRAGE

By the time the vote was won in 1920, Stanton and the four other women at that original tea party were dead. In fact, of all those who had signed the 1848 declaration, only Charlotte Woodward, who attended the conference as a nineteen-year-old, was alive to cast a ballot in the first election in which women could vote. In the years following that first convention, Stanton, along with her good friend Susan B. Anthony and others such as Lucy Stone and Sojourner Truth, criss-crossed the country lecturing, organizing, and rallying supporters to the cause. In time, universal suffrage emerged as the central issue, but in 1869 the women's movement fractured into two competing national organizations over the issue of whether to support ratification of the Fifteenth Amendment, which called for extending the vote to black men. Although most of those fighting for women's suffrage believed black people deserved the right to vote, some felt that admitting black men while leaving out all women would further entrench the attitude that men alone deserved the right to vote.

Frederick Douglass, the black abolitionist whose eloquence at the 1848 convention had helped sway the assembly to include the demand for women's suffrage, believed that black men needed the vote more than white women. This time, he employed his eloquence to argue that the Fifteenth Amendment deserved support:

> When women, because they are women, are hunted down through the cities of New York and New Orleans; when they are dragged from their houses and hung upon lamp posts; when their children are torn from their arms, and their brains are dashed upon the pavement; when they are objects of insult and outrage at every turn; when they are in danger of having their homes burnt down over their heads; when their children are not allowed to enter schools; then they will have an urgency to obtain the ballot equal to our own.

Against this, Stanton and Anthony argued that supporting the Fifteenth Amendment amounted to a constitutional acknowledgement of the superiority of men. As they saw it, "Every argument for the Negro is an argument for woman and no logician can escape it." Furthermore, they feared that if women missed out on being included in the Fifteenth Amendment, they would not get another chance for years. As Stanton wrote many years later: "The few who had the prescience to see the long years of apathy that always follow a great conflict, strained every nerve to settle the broad question of suffrage on its true basis while the people were still awake to its importance." Some black women agreed with Stanton, including Sojourner Truth, a former slave. In an 1867 speech, she argued,

There is a great stir about colored men getting their rights, but not a word about the colored women; and if colored men get their rights and not colored women theirs, the colored men will be masters over the women, and it will be just as bad as it was before. So I am for keeping the thing going while things are stirring; because if we wait till it is still, it will take a great while to get it going again.

In the end, the Fifteenth Amendment was ratified, and black men got the vote. The National Woman Suffrage Association, which had fought the ratification, and the American Woman Suffrage Association, which had supported it, worked largely independently of each other until 1890, when they were reconciled into a new organization. The National American Woman Suffrage Association adopted a new strategy that turned away from the traditional emphasis on connecting the rights of women with the rights of blacks. Instead, it focused almost exclusively on women's issues and tried to enlarge its membership by shedding its radical image. Finally, in June 1920, Congress approved the Nineteenth Amendment, which would give women the vote, and sent it to the states for ratification.

Thirty-six states needed to ratify the amendment before it became law, and by the summer of 1920 everything turned on a single state, Tennessee. From around the country, people for and against the amendment converged on Nashville, and in the end the state ratified it by a single vote: Harry Burn, a twenty-four-year-old member of the state assembly who had been advised by his mother in a telegram to "be a good boy," switched his vote at the last minute from no to yes. Explaining himself later, he said, "I know that a mother's advice is always safest for her boy to follow, and my mother wanted me to vote for ratification." The Nineteenth Amendment, affirming that the right of citizens to vote shall not be denied on account of sex, was officially added to the U.S. Constitution on August 26, 1920.

AFTER THE SUFFRAGE VICTORY

When the vote was won in 1920, much of the movement's momentum was lost. Although there had been some progress on the other issues discussed in the 1848 declaration, they had fallen into the background when the issue of suffrage came to the fore and, consequently, were easily forgotten when the suffrage battle was won. This is not to say, however, that nothing more was being done by feminist activists. In 1923 Alice Paul, the leader of the National Woman's Party, drafted an Equal Rights Amendment to the U.S. Constitution, which was to ensure that "men and women shall have equal rights throughout the United States and every place subject to its jurisdiction." Although Paul's efforts to get the amendment passed were unsuccessful, American feminists would continue her cause, reintroducing the proposed constitutional change in every session of Congress up to 1972, when it was finally passed. (It ultimately failed when not enough states ratified it.) In addition, as the fight for suffrage was drawing to a close, an issue not anticipated in the original declaration began to surface. Margaret Sanger, a nurse in New York City, led the call for reproductive freedom for women. Sanger, motivated by her experiences with poor families in New York's Lower East Side, believed that women's progress depended on their ability to control whether and when they had children. Too often, in Sanger's view, promising young women had their lives changed for the worse by unwanted pregnancies, and she sought to distribute birth control information, at the time considered obscene by U.S. law. Although several key legal battles were won during the 1930s, making it somewhat easier to get birth control, Sanger would have to wait until 1965 for the Supreme Court's decision in *Griswold v. Connecticut*, which made birth control legal for married couples in all states. (In 1972 in *Eisenstadt v. Baird*, the Supreme Court ruled that the right to privacy at the heart of the 1965 decision extended to unmarried couples as well.) Although Sanger's main concern was with birth control, she foreshadowed later feminists who would explicitly argue that full freedom for women included responsibility for their own sexuality.

IMPORTANT DECADES OF SOCIAL CHANGE

Although Paul, Sanger, and others were exceptions, for the most part the years between 1920, when suffrage was won, and the early 1960s, when the so-called Feminist Second Wave broke, were quiet years for the feminist movement. Women's organized political activity during these years was at a relative lull yet the political and social changes taking place had a huge effect on the nation's women and men. Between 1920 and 1960 came the Roaring Twenties, the Great Depression, World War II, and the postwar fifties. Each helped set in place the social conditions from which second-wave feminism later burst.

The Roaring Twenties took their name from the mood of excitement that accompanied the years following World War I—known then as "the War to End All Wars." As Americans moved to the cities in huge numbers, more women worked outside the home in industry, and, kindled by trends in music, fashion, and entertainment, a new attitude of openness settled over much of urban America. This period of prosperity and ease was abruptly shattered by the stock market crash of 1929 and the ensuing Great Depression, in which millions of Americans lost their jobs. In these destitute times, women often found themselves head of the family, thrust into trying situations that forced them to find and tap deep wells of strength, independence, and grit in order to survive. As well, the original American story—of new people in a new place facing new risks and opportunities—repeated itself during the vast migrations of the 1930s. As millions of American families moved around the country looking for work, particularly into the cities and toward the west, the traditional extended family became strained and more distant, and ties to traditional communities and their stabilizing patterns were weakened or lost. Many American families found themselves starting anew in unfamiliar places, an experience that, while difficult, ultimately helped them grow more comfortable with and adept at modifying or reinventing communities, social patterns, and ways of life. World War II, which broke over Europe in 1939 and drew America in two years later, also brought great change to American life. During the war, with huge numbers of American servicemen posted overseas, the employment of women boomed. Not only were there fewer men to fill the jobs, the massive war effort required increased industrial production and millions of women stepped in to help. Many, for the first time, got a taste of what it is like to earn their own money and found themselves amply capable in roles traditionally reserved for men. The end of the war, however, brought all this to a quick end. By 1948 most of the women had lost their jobs, often having been expressly fired in order to hire a man. By and large, society still expected men to earn the money and women to manage the house, and in the 1950s, American families, eager to leave the tragic years behind them, embraced these roles with enthusiasm. A postwar economic boom led to greater affluence, especially among white Americans, who responded by concentrating on home and family. Magazines promoted their ideal of American family life: a new home in the suburbs, a fine automobile, a gainfully employed husband accompanied by his pretty wife, the caring mother. For many Americans, for a few years at least, this was enough.

As the 1960s began, the sunny image of the 1950s prevailed. A handsome president and his beautiful wife took up residence in the White House in 1961, and there was a general mood of optimism about America's prospects. The decade would prove a fitful one, however: President John F. Kennedy, his brother Robert, and Martin Luther King Jr. were all assassinated; race riots broke out in the cities; a bloody war and counter demonstrations engulfed the nation; and—less violent but no less momentous—the modern women's movement emerged.

THE FEMINIST SECOND WAVE

The year 1963 is usually taken to mark the beginning of the second wave of U.S. feminism. During this year Betty Friedan published *The Feminine Mystique*, a book uncovering and exploring a malaise afflicting middle-class, educated white women in America. According to Friedan, the average homemaker, far from being a happy wife and a contented mother, felt herself intellectually and emotionally oppressed, stunted by the limited options society left open to her. Friedan also charged that the advertising industry and the leading women's magazines were responsible for inculcating and sustaining the myth of the happy housewife:

> It is their millions which blanket the land with persuasive images, flattering the American housewife, diverting her guilt and disguising her growing emptiness. They have done this so successfully, employing the techniques and concepts of modern social science, and transposing them into those deceptively simple, clever, outrageous ads and commercials, that an observer of the American scene today accepts as fact that the great majority of American women have no ambition other than to be housewives. If they are not responsible for sending women home, they are surely responsible for keeping them there.

The book became an instant best-seller and inspired thousands of women to look beyond home and family for fulfillment. During the fifteen years that followed the publication of Friedan's book, tremendous social and legal changes concerning women occurred in America. Although *The Feminine Mystique* is credited with boosting the feminist movement, its publication was as much a sign of the times as it was a catalyst.

The same year that *The Feminine Mystique* hit bookstores,

the Commission on the Status of Women, convened by President Kennedy in 1961, released the results of its comprehensive study. In what is commonly referred to as the Peterson Report, the commission catalogued discrimination against women in many corners of American life. The document made several recommendations, including that affordable child care be available for people of all incomes, that hiring practices promote equal opportunity for women, and that maternity leave be implemented. The chief effect of the report, however, may have been the numerous state commissions on the status of women that followed, through which women around the country turned their attention to women's issues. Also in 1963, the Equal Pay Act was passed into federal law, barring unequal pay for equal or substantially equal work performed by men and women within one company or organization.

THE MOVEMENT GAINS SPEED

Women's groups got a further boost the following year, when the Civil Rights Act was passed. This bill prohibited employment discrimination on the basis of race, religion, national origin, or sex. The category of sex was added as a last-minute amendment by Congressman Howard Smith of Virginia; he opposed civil rights legislation and thought Congress would reject a bill that provided for equal rights for women. Although the main target of the bill was racial discrimination, the Equal Employment Opportunity Commission, established to investigate discrimination complaints, received tens of thousands of sex discrimination complaints within its first few years. The main focus of the commission remained, however, investigating race-based complaints, and in 1966, annoyed at what was seen as a slow response by the government to sex discrimination, Friedan, along with other feminists active at state levels in the Commission on the Status of Women, founded the National Organization of Women (NOW). Friedan became the first president of this lobby group, which was modeled on the National Association for the Advancement of Colored People (NAACP). Many early second-wave feminists had been active in the civil rights movements of the 1950s and 1960s, in which the focus was fighting racial segregation and discrimination. Indeed, many second-wave feminists felt that their involvement in civil rights issues first alerted them to the discrimination they faced as women. For some, this was because they believed that involvement in the civil rights movements developed in them a heightened awareness to the role prejudice and stereotyping play in social organization. For others, though, the move to feminism was something they felt forced upon them by what they saw as sexism within civil rights organizations. Indeed, when women complained in 1964 about being kept out of leadership positions in the Student Non-Violent Coordinating Committee, a civil rights activist group, they did not get quite the reaction for which they had been hoping. Stokely Carmichael, one of the group's leaders, famously remarked, "The only position for women in the SNCC is prone."

In the late nineteenth century the women's liberation movement was created, beginning with the fight for women's suffrage.

The NAACP, after which NOW was modeled, had historically included both black and white people. Similarly, NOW was to include men and was, according to its founding statement of purpose, to work "toward a fully equal partnership of the sexes." Although NOW was the largest and most visible feminist organization in the United States, equally important to the movement were the hundreds of small grassroots organizations that sprang up around the country. While the national organization was capturing headlines and winning court battles, small groups of women meeting on campuses and in cafés, bookstores, and living rooms were discussing the changes they envisioned unfolding in society. They founded feminist newspapers, opened women's shelters and rape crisis centers, pioneered women-specific health services, and provided a more familiar, local face to feminism.

RUNNING INTO RESISTANCE

By the late 1960s few Americans had not noticed that—for better or for worse, as opinions varied—a lot was changing. Although many people, including men, agreed with NOW and other feminist groups, others thought feminism was a destructive influence, destabilizing time-honored traditions and familiar ways of life. One dramatic example of this occurred at the 1967 Boston Marathon, the venerable sporting event that at the time was closed to women. Kathrine Switzer, who was eager to run what most considered the world's premiere marathon but was barred because of her sex, registered using only her first initial. Race organizers assumed she was a man and sent her a race number. Partway through the 26.2-mile race, the race director, Jock Semple, outraged at seeing a woman running with an official race number, tried to tackle Switzer. She managed to elude him, however, and finished the marathon successfully. Although in later years Semple warmed up to the idea of women participating in the Boston Marathon, at the time he was not alone in finding feminism a harmful influence.

EQUALITY BEFORE THE LAW

During the 1960s and 1970s the level of feminist interest and activism was unprecedented, and feminists won many battles in the courtroom and in the public eye. By 1977 the Supreme

Court had issued no less than twenty-two full decisions in cases considered women's rights cases by feminist activists. But many other legal changes occurred at lower court levels or in state and national legislatures.

Some of the most significant legal changes concerned the employment of women and the access by women to public resources. In 1965 the Equal Employment Opportunity Commission's first ruling on a discrimination charge held that corporate policies that mandated the firing of female employees when they marry violates Title VII of the Civil Rights Act. In 1968 the commission made it clear that the common practice of having separate help-wanted advertisements for men and women likewise violated Title VII, and this was upheld by the Supreme Court in 1973. In *Weeks v. Southern Bell* (1969) and *Rosenfeld v. Southern Pacific* (1971) two federal courts of appeal adopted the commission's view (which it had filed in amicus briefs), striking down state laws that limited the kinds of jobs women could hold. The state laws concerned had been known as protective laws, stipulating the hours and conditions under which women were allowed to work. The commission had argued that these stipulations in practice were used to discriminate against and exclude women from jobs. On appeal, the Fifth Circuit rebuked Southern Bell for relying in its legal arguments on stereotypes concerning men and women, and, in particular, for arguing that women should be excluded from certain jobs on the grounds that those jobs are unpleasant:

> Title VII rejects just this type of romantic paternalism as unduly Victorian and instead vests individual women with the power to decide if they should take on unromantic tasks. Men have always had the right to determine whether the incremental increase in remuneration for strenuous, dangerous, obnoxious, boring or unromantic tasks is worth the candle. The promise of Title VII is that women are now to be on an equal footing.

In 1971 the Supreme Court ruled in *Reed v. Reed* that a state law favoring men violated the Fourteenth Amendment, which guarantees citizens equal protection under the law. The case, which was argued by present Supreme Court justice Ruth Bader Ginsburg, concerned an Idaho man who died without a will. Both of his parents, who were separated, asked to be administrators of his estate, and both were found to be equally qualified. Idaho law, however, required that if all other factors are equal, "males must be preferred to females." Chief Justice Warren Burger wrote in the decision,

> We have concluded the arbitrary preference established in favor of males cannot stand in the face of the Fourteenth Amendment's command that no State deny the equal protection of the laws to any person. To give a mandatory preference to members of either sex is to make the very kind of arbitrary legislative choice forbidden by the Equal Protection Clause.

In 1972 Title IX, included in the Education Code of 1972, guaranteed women equal access to higher education. Although the new law contributed to a boom in the number of female doctors, lawyers, engineers, and other professionals, it had an equally dramatic impact on athletic programs at high schools and universities. According to Title IX, schools and universities could not discriminate in the amount of money they spent on athletic programs for males and for females. For many feminists, female involvement in sports was crucial to dispelling old notions of female fragility.

In 1973 the Supreme Court ruled in *Cleveland Board of Education v. LaFleur* that requiring pregnant women to take maternity leave on the assumption that their physical condition would impair their teaching ability violates the Equal Protection Clause. In 1974 the Equal Credit Opportunity Act made it illegal to discriminate in consumer credit practices on the basis of race, color, religion, national origin, sex, marital status, age (as long as the lender is old enough to sign contracts), or receipt of welfare. The law was extended to include commercial lending in 1989. In 1975 the Supreme Court ruled in *Taylor v. Louisiana* that states do not have the right to exclude

women from juries. The Supreme Court ruling, which over-
turned the Louisiana Supreme Court's finding, held that the
systematic exclusion of women violates the Sixth Amendment
guarantee that a jury be drawn from a representative cross-
section of the community:

> The purpose of a jury is to guard against the exercise of ar-
> bitrary power—to make available the commonsense judg-
> ment of the community as a hedge against the overzealous
> or mistaken prosecutor and in preference to the professional
> or perhaps over-conditioned or biased response of a judge.
> This prophylactic vehicle is not provided if the jury pool is
> made up of only special segments of the populace or if
> large, distinctive groups are excluded from the pool. Com-
> munity participation in the administration of the criminal
> law, moreover, is not only consistent with our democratic
> heritage but is also critical to public confidence in the fair-
> ness of the criminal justice system. Restricting jury service
> to only special groups or excluding identifiable segments
> playing major roles in the community cannot be squared
> with the constitutional concept of jury trial.

The courts were making clear that the law was to treat men
and women equally.

LAW AND FAMILY LIFE

In addition to legal changes that concerned largely employment issues and other issues in the public sphere, there were
numerous legal changes more intimately connected to private
life, such as those that concerned contraception, abortion, and
family law. In 1969 California put into place the first "no-
fault" divorce law, which allowed couples to divorce with mutual consent, and other states soon followed California's lead.
In 1973 the Supreme Court in *Roe v. Wade* effectively wiped
out the antiabortion laws in forty-six states by ruling that such
laws interfere with a woman's right to private control of her
body. In 1976 Nebraska law made marital rape illegal, the first
time it was recognized that a man has no legal right to have
sex with his wife against her will. In 1978, in the wake of pub-

licity about the *Oregon v. Rideout* decision, in which a husband was found not guilty of raping his wife, many other states began allowing prosecution for marital and cohabitation rape.

THE PERSONAL IS POLITICAL

Although much of the change during the 1960s and 1970s occurred in the public sphere—the introduction of new laws and the discarding of old ones, for instance—the structure of personal life was beginning to change, too. Indeed, the second-wave feminists introduced the slogan "the Personal Is Political," which was meant to reflect their belief that there was not a clear divide between the personal and political spheres. They insisted that the content and the character of people's personal lives is not just an issue of personal preferences and choices. Rather, such personal lives are limited, shaped, and defined by the broader political and social setting surrounding a person. This idea, which was central to second-wave feminism, meant that feminists did not rest with criticizing and trying to change what they considered unjust laws and legal structures. There was also a strong emphasis on examining one's own life with an eye to seeing the ways in which it had been influenced and ordered by prevailing, perhaps unjust, social customs.

With this in mind, one of the important distinctions feminist thinkers introduced was that between sex and gender. According to this distinction, a person's sex (male or female) was determined by genetics, whereas a person's gender (masculine or feminine) was shaped by social influences. Thus, for instance, the fact that some human beings have male reproductive organs and some have female reproductive organs is simply a question of genetics, whereas the fact that there seem to be masculine and feminine personality traits is a result of social forces. If it is true that men tend to be more aggressive, more competitive, and less emotional, according to this argument, this is because they have been raised in a society that encourages them to be that way. The categories of "men" and "women," it was argued, are thus artificial categories, at least in so far as they are categories that suggest different social characteristics. The degree to which people's characteristics are determined by their genetics or by their social conditioning remains very controversial, but the distinction feminists introduced between sex and gender remains influential in these discussions.

For some women actively involved in the feminist movement, examining the relationship between the personal and the political led them to believe that relationships between men and women were based on a power dynamic in which women were subordinate to men. Some feminists came to argue that it was not possible for women to have genuine romantic or sexual relationships with men because of this inequality. The idea was that as long as men have power over women, women cannot genuinely consent to a relationship with a man because any alleged consent would be nothing other than coercion. Furthermore, it was argued, in a society that values men more highly than women, feminists have a duty to exalt and cherish other women. To do so, it was believed, was to resist the oppressive forces that tell women they should direct their affection and admiration toward men. Such considerations, among others, led to the development of what was known variously as radical feminism, feminist separatism, and lesbian separatism. Many feminists believed that rather than fighting to be an equal partner in a man's world, women would be better off living amongst themselves. In communities of women, it was argued, women would be true equals and treated as such. Furthermore, within such communities women were to have the best chances for finding enduring intellectual, emotional, and sexual fulfilment. Not everyone was fond of this idea, however, and there was great controversy over the degree to which such considerations should make it into the public agenda of feminist organizations.

AN IDEA TAKES ROOT

The feminist emphasis on the importance of the idea that the personal is political, of course, did not always lead to so-called radical feminism. The idea took root just as firmly in feminists opposed or even hostile to the more radical aspects of feminism and is one of feminism's enduring contributions to contemporary American life. In affirming that there is no firm division between the personal and political, feminists charged Americans with the task of recognizing the connections between their personal lives and the politics of their societies. Originally, this meant recognizing that the character of personal lives was determined in part by the political and social setting in which one lived. Later, however, the idea that the personal is political came to have a different, yet related, meaning. According to this second interpretation, the political structure of a society is determined by the personal choices and decisions of individual members of the society. Individuals were thus charged with the responsibility of living their personal lives in ways that would help create the society in which they wished to live. These two interpretations of the idea that the personal is political are related in affirming that there are deep connections between the personal and political, and it was second-wave feminism that was largely responsible for making them part of the fabric of contemporary American thought.

A MOVEMENT IN TROUBLE?

By the end of the 1970s many feminists and observers felt that the women's movement in America was in trouble. It was not that there was less activism or interest, nor was it thought that there were no more battles to be won. The problem, instead, was that the united front that feminists presented through the 1960s was beginning to fracture. The main issue that motivated early second-wave feminists—most of whom were white, middle-class, and educated—was discrimination in employment, education, and family life. Not everyone welcomed the introduction of lesbian issues to the feminist agenda, and some of the first divisions in the movement occurred between those who saw such issues as central to feminists and those who saw them as distracting or even dangerous to the movement. By the late 1970s another major source of tension was a concern about racism and classism among feminist leaders. Many black, and later Latino, feminists felt that they had distinct concerns that were not always in accord with those of their white feminist colleagues. In addition, many black feminists felt excluded from the power centers of prominent feminist organizations, which were dominated by white women.

The response from white feminists tended to go in one of two directions. Some white feminists chose not to adapt or respond to the issues raised by their black colleagues, which contributed to an even greater sense of alienation among black feminists. Equally common, however, was a quite different response. Many white feminists came to believe that they had harbored prejudices against nonwhite people, prejudices that had affected their thought and behavior in ways in which they had not been aware. Such considerations led many white feminists to rethink their attitudes toward men, who had often been thought to be knowing and willing participants in sexist systems of oppression. For many white feminists, the revelation that they themselves had unwittingly held racist attitudes and participated in racist systems of oppression brought a new complexity to their feminist views. For many, clear-cut distinctions between good and bad, oppressed and oppressor, were no longer tenable. Rather, many feminist thinkers maintained, each individual is situated in a complex social position, enjoying various advantages and suffering various disadvantages in virtue of such factors as sex, race, age, class, education, and so on.

A CHANGING AGENDA

Although few of the women and men who had been active in feminist causes during the 1960s and 1970s disavowed the importance of ending sexual discrimination, as the 1980s began the complexity of race, class, and other diverse aspects of individual identity loomed. It soon became unclear what agenda remained that was distinctly feminist or what cause could draw together women in all their diversity. In time, sexual issues emerged as the main feminist concern of the 1980s. Increasingly, feminists targeted sexual assault, sexual harassment, pornography, and prostitution as social ills that victimized women. Although sexual assault found few defenders, more controversial were feminist claims about the prevalence and ubiquitousness of sexual assault. Feminists insisted that sexual assault was very common and in particular that the most common sexual assault was what came to be called date rape. Feminists insisted that a man coercing his date for sex was wrong—that no means no—and that a man's continuing advances despite a woman's rejoinders to stop was sexual assault. Similarly, feminists insisted that sexual overtures in the workplace—especially those that involve unwelcome touching or invitations—constituted sexual harassment.

Many feminists, led by the legal scholar Catherine McKinnon, pegged pornography as a key instrument in the oppression of women. According to their arguments, pornography depicts women as sexual objects alone, contributing to a social view in which women are to serve and satisfy men. Thus, as they understood it, pornography harms all women. The sex industry at large, including prostitution, was targeted as an industry dominated by men making their fortunes by exploiting young women, many of whom were forced into or kept in the business through coercion, threats, abuse, or desperation. This new feminist focus was not uncontroversial, however. Some, such as Betty Friedan, thought the focus on sexual issues distracted feminists from the economic issues that lay at the core of the 1960s' feminist agenda and was out of touch with the lives of most American women. But others felt that feminist thinkers were simply of the wrong opinion on the issues they did raise. Some people thought feminist thinkers were overreacting to date rape and sexual harassment and complained about what they saw as an attempt to legislate on the delicate manners of courtship. Perhaps more prominently, though, not everyone, and especially not all feminists, agreed that pornography and prostitution were bad for women. Some feminists argued that pornography and prostitution were means by which women could gain power and influence, and pornography, in particular, was argued to be a potentially useful means by which women could explore and develop their own sexuality. Feminists continued to be united, of course, in their desire to improve the situation of women, but they were divided to the extent to which they held competing views of what would best achieve that.

THE FEMINIST THIRD WAVE

As the 1990s opened, there was much controversy over the state of the women's movement in America and competing interpretations of its present role and status. To most, it was clear that the women's movement was no longer one united force, as it had been during the 1960s, capable of dominating political agendas and the media limelight. Many took this as a sign of the movement's decline or as a testimony to its irrelevance. Yet for others the absence of one concerted women's movement was a sign of success. According to this second line of argument, there was no longer such a thing as "the" women's movement in America only because feminism and feminist concerns had grown too widespread and diverse to fall under any one category. Far from being dead, according to this view, the movement had simply shifted form, permeating society at various levels and in various ways.

The generation that reached adulthood in the 1990s was the first that grew up after the big women's movements battles of the 1960s and 1970s had been won. For most in that generation, the idea of a female doctor, lawyer, engineer, or even soldier was not all that unusual, nor was there an almost universal assumption, as there had been decades earlier, that every woman would become a wife and a mother. It was in these years that one started to hear of third-wave feminism, a new term that suggested that during the 1990s feminists shifted emphasis or tactics significantly enough to be seen as descendants, rather than as sisters, of the second-wave feminists.

Third-wave feminism has drawn some criticism from feminists active during the 1960s and 1970s, who often think the younger generation does not heed the lessons of its elders. In particular, many have been dismayed by the emphasis on "girl power," which often includes a sexy or saucy edge, as exemplified by the Spice Girls, that some suggest is a retreat to gender stereotypes. As well, third wavers are seen to be less cerebral, more interested in celebration than in developing a critical understanding of the power structures in which they are entwined. This theoretical undertaking was a chief activity among feminists during the 1960s and 1970s, owing in part to that movement's origins in the university-educated upper-middleclass. Third wavers, in contrast, are a more diverse group and hold this up as one of their strengths. As Rebecca Walker put it in her 1995 book *To Be Real: Telling the Truth and Changing the Face of Feminism,* "For many of us it seems that to be a feminist in the way that we have seen or understood feminism is to conform to an identity and way of living that doesn't allow for individuality, complexity or less than perfect personal histories." The idea is that whereas feminists of a generation ago had a fairly well-developed party line, adequately supported by a theoretical framework, the present generation of young women (and men) who make up the third wave are less likely and less willing to have a shared code of beliefs. The contrast can be seen, for instance, in attitudes toward sado-masochistic sexuality. Some young women are interested in experimenting with sado-masochism, believing it to be one means among many of exploring their sexuality and themselves. A core feminist principle of many second wavers, however, is that the synthesis of sex and violence, or of sex and pain, perpetuates violence against women and the oppression of women. Such occasional antagonisms between second- and third-wave feminists have not stopped, however, the development of successful intergenerational feminist organizations.

One other issue that rose to prominence during the 1990s was the relationships between American feminism and women around the world. Although international efforts within the women's movement date back to the days of the suffrage campaign, during the 1990s feminist activists increasingly started to concentrate on the situation of women outside the United States, particularly in the developing world. They drew attention to the unequal legal treatment of women in many countries of the world, and to such practices as female circumcision and the sale and trafficking of women into sexual slavery. In particular, feminists within the United States and other wealthy industrialized countries provided funding and organizational experience to nongovernmental organizations abroad. At the same time, however, some feminist thinkers expressed concern that as more American women became successful in business and industry, they became part of an unjust economic system that contributes to the poverty and exploitation of women in foreign countries. Once again, feminists were united in agreeing on the importance of improving the status of women, wherever they were to be found, but disagreed on the means by which to achieve this goal.

This theme of conflict within the feminist movement is a recurring one, reaching back to the days of the suffrage movement, when the two major national women's organizations disagreed on whether to support the constitutional amendment that called for extending the vote to black men alone. Although feminism has sometimes been criticized or even belittled for having such internal conflicts, most feminists answer that there is nothing wrong with feminists having different opinions on important issues. Furthermore, the history of feminism, like that of most social movements, is not so much the story of one band of people united by a rigidly shared set of beliefs as it is a story of various groups of people, sharing a rich new insight, setting about in diverse ways to investigate and achieve the future they believe that insight promises.

ABSTRACT IDEAS AND INTIMATE LIVES

The history of feminism is thus a history of ideas—the foremost among them that women are the intellectual and moral equals of men—as much as it is a history of events. Yet ultimately, perhaps, the most important developments of all occurred in the personal lives of individuals. As the historian Carol Hymowitz points out, feminism intimately touched the lives of all Americans, male and female: "Feminists asked men and women to think of themselves in new ways and to relate differently to each other. If wives, mothers, daughters changed, husbands, fathers, and sons would be called upon to change as well."

Although many men shared the view of Jock Semple, the director of the Boston Marathon who became outraged upon seeing a woman running the race, many other men embraced feminism and the changes it brought to their lives. Large numbers of men participated in feminist organizations, and even more tried to integrate feminist perspectives into their personal and public lives. Rather than seeing a natural antagonism between feminism and men, many joined with feminists in concentrating on initiatives that helped women, such as the founding of organizations that tried to end male violence against women. Furthermore, many men came to share the view that most differences between men and women are the result of the society in which one lives, and they welcomed the chance to discard traditional masculine or macho models of behavior.

Although many men embraced feminism and the changes it brought to their lives, it would be a mistake to overestimate the degree to which men welcomed the women's movement. For that matter, it would be a mistake to overestimate the degree to which women themselves welcomed the movement that presumed to speak for them. Many women, as far back as the days of suffrage, resented what they saw as feminist intrusions into established and honored patterns of life. Hymowitz argues that this hostility to feminism, as she calls it, is due to the fact that feminism was unique among social movements in asking for personal change: "Other reform movements could be embraced abstractly; they called on people to change the world. The women's rights movement made people angry and frightened because it asked them to change themselves." Whether or not one agrees with Hymowitz that those who resisted feminism did so because the movement asked them to change their own lives rather than the world, there can be little doubt that feminism has changed both the personal lives of Americans and the world in which those lives are lived.

CHAPTER 1

RIGHTS AND REASON: AMERICAN WOMEN WIN THE VOTE

AMERICAN
SOCIAL
MOVEMENTS

Declaration of Sentiments

ELIZABETH CADY STANTON, SUSAN B. ANTHONY,
AND MATILDA JOSLYN GAGE

The six-volume *History of Woman Suffrage*, published in 1881 by Elizabeth Cady Stanton, Susan B. Anthony, and Matilda Joslyn Gage,
chronicles the first 30 years of the suffragist movement in America.
The following selection is drawn from the first volume of this work,
and documents the first women's rights convention, held in Seneca
Falls, New York, in 1848. At that convention Stanton read the *Declaration of Sentiments and Resolutions*, which was modeled on the *Declaration of Independence* and outlined a set of grievances and demands
for change. The following selection describes the origins of that declaration, its discussion and adoption at the convention, and the public response to it. The three authors were all prominent leaders in
the suffrage movement, but none lived to see the ratification of the
constitutional amendment guaranteeing women the right to vote.

The *Seneca County Courier,* a semi-weekly journal, of July
14, 1848, contained the following startling announcement:

SENECA FALLS CONVENTION.

WOMAN'S RIGHTS CONVENTION.—A Convention to discuss the social, civil, and religious condition and rights of
woman, will be held in the Wesleyan Chapel, at Seneca
Falls, N.Y., on Wednesday and Thursday, the 19th and 20th
of July, current; commencing at 10 o'clock A.M. During the
first day the meeting will be exclusively for women, who
are earnestly invited to attend. The public generally are in-

Excerpted from *History of Women's Suffrage, Vol. 1,* by Elizabeth Cady Stanton, Susan B.
Anthony, and Matilda Joslyn Gage (New York: Fowler & Wells, 1881).

vited to be present on the second day, when Lucretia Mott, of Philadelphia, and other ladies and gentlemen, will address the convention.

This call, without signature, was issued by Lucretia Mott, Martha C. Wright, Elizabeth Cady Stanton, and Mary Ann McClintock. . . . These four ladies, sitting round the tea-table of Richard Hunt, a prominent Friend near Waterloo, decided to put their long-talked-of resolution into action, and before the twilight deepened into night, the call was written, and sent to the *Seneca County Courier.* On Sunday morning they met in Mrs. McClintock's parlor to write their declaration, resolutions, and to consider subjects for speeches. As the convention was to assemble in three days, the time was short for such productions; but having no experience in the *modus operandi* of getting up conventions, nor in that kind of literature, they were quite innocent of the herculean labors they proposed. On the first attempt to frame a resolution; to crowd a complete thought, clearly and concisely, into three lines; they felt as helpless and hopeless as if they had been suddenly asked to construct a steam engine. And the humiliating fact may as well now be recorded that before taking the initiative step, those ladies resigned themselves to a faithful perusal of various masculine productions. The reports of Peace, Temperance, and Anti-Slavery conventions were examined, but all alike seemed too tame and pacific for the inauguration of a rebellion such as the world had never before seen. They knew women had wrongs, but how to state them was the difficulty, and this was increased from the fact that they themselves were fortunately organized and conditioned; they were neither "sour old maids," "childless women," nor "divorced wives," as the newspapers declared them to be. While they had felt the insults incident to sex, in many ways, as every proud, thinking woman must, in the laws, religion, and literature of the world, and in the invidious and degrading sentiments and customs of all nations, yet they had not in their own experience endured the coarser forms of tyranny resulting from unjust laws, or association with immoral and unscrupulous men, but they had souls large enough to feel the wrongs of others, without being scarified in their own flesh.

THE DECLARATION OF INDEPENDENCE SERVES AS A MODEL

After much delay, one of the circle took up the Declaration of 1776, and read it aloud with much spirit and emphasis, and it was at once decided to adopt the historic document, with some slight changes such as substituting "all men" for "King George." Knowing that women must have more to complain of than men under any circumstances possibly could, and seeing the Fathers had eighteen grievances, a protracted search was made through statute books, church usages, and the customs of society to find that exact number. Several well-disposed men assisted in collecting the grievances, until, with the announcement of the eighteenth, the women felt they had enough to go before the world with a good case. One youthful lord remarked, "Your grievances must be grievous indeed, when you are obliged to go to books in order to find them out."

The eventful day dawned at last, and crowds in carriages and on foot, wended their way to the Wesleyan church. . . .

The Declaration having been freely discussed by many present, was re-read by Mrs. Stanton, and with some slight amendments adopted.

DECLARATION OF SENTIMENTS

When, in the course of human events, it becomes necessary for one portion of the family of man to assume among the people of the earth a position different from that which they have hitherto occupied, but one to which the laws of nature and of nature's God entitle them, a decent respect to the opinions of mankind requires that they should declare the causes that impel them to such a course.

We hold these truths to be self-evident: that all men and women are created equal; that they are endowed by their Creator with certain inalienable rights; that among these are life, liberty, and the pursuit of happiness; that to secure these rights governments are instituted, deriving their just powers from the consent of the governed. Whenever any form of government becomes destructive of these ends, it is the right of those who suffer from it to refuse allegiance to it, and to insist upon the institution of a new government, laying its foundation on such principles, and organizing its powers in such form, as to them shall seem most likely to effect their safety and happiness. Prudence indeed, will dictate that governments long established should not be changed for light and transient causes; and accordingly all experience hath shown that mankind are more disposed to suffer, while evils are sufferable, than to right themselves by abolishing the forms to which they were accustomed. But when a long train of abuses and usurpations, pursuing invariably the same object evinces a design to reduce them under absolute despotism, it is their duty to throw off such government, and to provide new guards for their future security. Such has been the patient sufferance of the women under this government, and such is now the necessity which constrains them to demand the equal station to which they are entitled.

A List of Grievances

The history of mankind is a history of repeated injuries and usurpations on the part of man toward woman, having in direct object the establishment of an absolute tyranny over her. To prove this, let facts be submitted to a candid world.

He has never permitted her to exercise her inalienable right to the elective franchise.

He has compelled her to submit to laws, in the formation of which she had no voice.

He has withheld from her rights which are given to the most ignorant and degraded men—both natives and foreigners.

Having deprived her of this first right of a citizen, the elective franchise, thereby leaving her without representation in the halls of legislation, he has oppressed her on all sides.

He has made her, if married, in the eye of the law, civilly dead.

He has taken from her all right in property, even to the wages she earns.

He has made her, morally, an irresponsible being, as she can commit many crimes with impunity, provided they be done in the presence of her husband. In the covenant of marriage, she is compelled to promise obedience to her husband, he becoming, to all intents and purposes, her master—the law giving him power to deprive her of her liberty, and to administer chastisement.

He has so framed the laws of divorce, as to what shall be the proper causes, and in case of separation, to whom the guardianship of the children shall be given, as to be wholly regardless of the happiness of women—the law, in all cases, going upon a false supposition of the supremacy of man, and giving all power into his hands.

After depriving her of all rights as a married woman, if single, and the owner of property, he has taxed her to support a government which recognizes her only when her property can be made profitable to it.

He has monopolized nearly all the profitable employments, and from those she is permitted to follow, she receives but a scanty remuneration. He closes against her all the avenues to wealth and distinction which he considers most honorable to himself. As a teacher of theology, medicine, or law, she is not known.

He has denied her the facilities for obtaining a thorough education, all colleges being closed against her.

He allows her in Church, as well as State, but a subordinate position, claiming Apostolic authority for her exclusion from the ministry, and, with some exceptions, from any public participation in the affairs of the Church.

He has created a false public sentiment by giving to the world a different code of morals for men and women, by which moral delinquencies which exclude women from society, are not only tolerated, but deemed of little account in man.

He has usurped the prerogative of Jehovah himself, claiming it as his right to assign for her a sphere of action, when that belongs to her conscience and to her God.

He has endeavored, in every way that he could, to destroy her confidence in her own powers, to lessen her self-respect, and to make her willing to lead a dependent and abject life.

Now, in view of this entire disfranchisement of one-half the people of this country, their social and religious degradation—in view of the unjust laws above mentioned, and because women do feel themselves aggrieved, oppressed, and fraudulently deprived of their most sacred rights, we insist that they have immediate admission to all the rights and privileges which belong to them as citizens of the United States.

In entering upon the great work before us, we anticipate no small amount of misconception, misrepresentation, and ridicule; but we shall use every instrumentality within our power to effect our object. We shall employ agents, circulate tracts, petition the State and National legislatures, and endeavor to enlist the pulpit and the press in our behalf. We hope this Convention will be followed by a series of Conventions embracing every part of the country.

Resolutions for Change

The following resolutions were discussed by Lucretia Mott, Thomas and Mary Ann McClintock, Amy Post, Catharine A.F. Stebbins, and others, and were adopted:

> WHEREAS, The great precept of nature is conceded to be, that "man shall pursue his own true and substantial happiness." Blackstone in his Commentaries remarks, that this law of Nature being coeval with mankind, and dictated by God himself, is of course superior in obligation to any other. It is binding over all the globe, in all countries and at all times; no human laws are of any validity if contrary to this, and such of them as are valid, derive all their force, and all their validity, and all their authority, mediately and immediately, from this original; therefore,
>
> *Resolved,* That such laws as conflict, in any way, with the true and substantial happiness of woman, are contrary to the

great precept of nature and of no validity, for this is "superior in obligation to any other."

Resolved, That all laws which prevent woman from occupying such a station in society as her conscience shall dictate, or which place her in position inferior to that of man, are contrary to the great precept of nature, and therefore of no force or authority.

Resolved, That woman is man's equal—was intended to be so by the Creator, and the highest good of the race demands that she should be recognized as such.

Resolved, That the women of this country ought to be enlightened in regard to the laws under which they live, that they may no longer publish their degradation by declaring themselves satisfied with their present position, nor their ignorance, by asserting that they have all the rights they want.

Resolved, That inasmuch as man, while claiming for himself intellectual superiority, does accord to woman moral superiority, it is pre-eminently his duty to encourage her to speak and teach, as she has an opportunity, in all religious assemblies.

Resolved, That the same amount of virtue, delicacy, and refinement of behavior that is required of woman in the social state, should also be required of man, and the same transgressions should be visited with equal severity on both man and woman.

Resolved, That the objection of indelicacy and impropriety, which is so often brought against woman when she addresses a public audience, comes with a very ill-grace from those who encourage, by their attendance, her appearance on the stage, in the concert, or in feats of the circus.

Resolved, That woman has too long rested satisfied in the circumscribed limits which corrupt customs and a perverted application of the Scriptures have marked out for her, and that it is time she should move in the enlarged sphere which her great Creator has assigned her.

Resolved, That it is the duty of the women of this country to secure to themselves their sacred right to the elective franchise.

Resolved, That the equality of human rights results necessarily from the fact of the identity of the race in capabilities and responsibilities.

Resolved, therefore, That, being invested by the Creator with the same capabilities, and the same consciousness of responsibility for their exercise, it is demonstrably the right and duty of woman, equally with man, to promote every righteous cause by every righteous means; and especially in regard to the great subjects of morals and religion, it is self-evidently her right to participate with her brother in teaching them, both in private and in public, by writing and by speaking, by any instrumentalities proper to be used, and in any assemblies proper to be held; and this being a self-evident truth growing out of the divinely implanted principles of human nature, any custom or authority adverse to it, whether modern or wearing the hoary sanction of antiquity, is to be regarded as a self-evident falsehood, and at war with mankind.

At the last session Lucretia Mott offered and spoke to the following resolution:

Resolved, That the speedy success of our cause depends upon the zealous and untiring efforts of both men and women, for the overthrow of the monopoly of the pulpit, and for the securing to woman an equal participation with men in the various trades, professions, and commerce.

A CONTROVERSY OVER SUFFRAGE

The only resolution that was not unanimously adopted was the ninth, urging the women of the country to secure to themselves the elective franchise. Those who took part in the debate feared a demand for the right to vote would defeat others they deemed more rational, and make the whole movement ridiculous.

But Mrs. Stanton and Frederick Douglass seeing that the power to choose rulers and make laws, was the right by which all others could be secured, persistently advocated the resolution, and at last carried it by a small majority.

Thus it will be seen that the Declaration and resolutions in the very first Convention, demanded all the most radical friends of the movement have since claimed—such as equal rights in the universities, in the trades and professions; the right to vote; to share in all political offices, honors, and emoluments; to complete equality in marriage, to personal freedom, property, wages, children; to make contracts; to sue, and be sued; and to testify in courts of justice. At this time the condition of married women under the Common Law, was nearly as degraded as that of the slave on the Southern plantation. The Convention continued through two entire days, and late into the evenings. The deepest interest was manifested to its close.

AN ANGRY REACTION

The proceedings were extensively published, unsparingly ridiculed by the press, and denounced by the pulpit, much to the surprise and chagrin of the leaders. Being deeply in earnest, and believing their demands pre-eminently wise and just, they were wholly unprepared to find themselves the target for the jibes and jeers of the nation. The Declaration was signed by one hundred men, and women, many of whom withdrew their names as soon as the storm of ridicule began to break. The comments of the press were carefully preserved, and it is curious to see that the same old arguments, and objections rife at the start, are reproduced by the press of to-day. But the brave protests sent out from this Convention touched a responsive chord in the hearts of women all over the country.

Conventions were held soon after in Ohio, Massachusetts, Indiana, Pennsylvania, and at different points in New York.

A VOICE OF SUPPORT

Mr. Douglass, in his paper, *The North Star,* of July 28, 1848, had the following editorial leader:

THE RIGHTS OF WOMEN.—One of the most interesting events of the past week, was the holding of what is technically styled a Woman's Rights Convention at Seneca Falls. The speaking, addresses, and resolutions of this extraordinary meeting were almost wholly conducted by women; and although they evidently felt themselves in a novel position, it is but simple justice to say that their whole proceedings were characterized by marked ability and dignity. No one present, we think, however much he might be disposed to differ from the views advanced by the leading speakers on that occasion, will fail to give them credit for brilliant talents and excellent dispositions. In this meeting, as in other deliberative assemblies, there were frequent differences of opinion and animated discussion; but in no case was there the slightest absence of good feeling and decorum. Several interesting documents setting forth the rights as well as grievances of women were read. Among these was a Declaration of Sentiments, to be regarded as the basis of a grand movement for attaining the civil, social, political, and religious rights of women. We should not do justice to our own convictions, or to the excellent persons connected with this infant movement, if we did not in this connection offer a few remarks on the general subject which the Convention met to consider and the objects they seek to attain. In doing so, we are not insensible that the bare mention of this truly important subject in any other than terms of contemptuous ridicule and scornful disfavor, is likely to excite against us the fury of bigotry and the folly of prejudice. A discussion of the rights of animals would be regarded with far more complacency by many of what are called the *wise* and the *good* of our land, than would be a discussion of the rights of women. It is, in their estimation, to be guilty of evil thoughts, to think that woman is entitled to equal rights with man. Many who have at last made the discovery that the negroes have some rights as well as other members of the human family, have yet to be convinced that women are entitled to any. Eight years ago a number of persons of this description actually abandoned the anti-slavery cause, lest by giving their influence in that direction they might possibly be giving countenance to the dangerous heresy that woman, in respect to rights, stands on an equal footing with man. In the judgment of such persons the American slave system, with all its concomitant horrors, is less to be deplored than this *wicked* idea. It is perhaps needless to say, that we cherish little sympathy for such sentiments or respect for such prejudices. Standing as we do upon the watch-tower of human freedom, we can not be deterred from an expression of our approbation of any movement, however humble, to improve and elevate the character of any members of the human family. While it is impossible for us to go into this subject at length, and dispose of the various objections which are often urged against such a doctrine as that of female equality, we are free to say that in respect to political rights, we hold woman to be justly entitled to all we claim for man. We go farther, and express our conviction that all political rights which it is expedient for man to exercise, it is equally so for woman. All that distinguishes man as an intelligent and accountable being, is equally true of woman; and if that government only is just which governs by the free consent of the governed, there can be no reason in the world for denying to woman the exercise of the elective franchise, or a hand in making and administering the laws of the land. Our doctrine is that "right is of no sex." We therefore bid the women engaged in this movement our humble Godspeed.

The Emergence of Women's Rights as a Political Issue

Sheila Tobias is an author and science education consultant with a background in post-secondary education initiatives. In this selection, drawn from her 1997 book *Faces of Feminism*, she explores the origins of the feminist movement in the United States. Tobias argues that the roots of the movement lay in women's participation in three other reform movements of the nineteenth century. Tobias points to women's prominent roles in the temperance movement, which fought alcohol consumption, in the antislavery movement, which sought freedom for black Americans, and in a reformist tradition which helped poor, mentally ill, and immigrant Americans. Experience in these movements, Tobias argues, developed women's capacities for political involvement and demonstrated to them their need for political equality. At the end of the selection, Tobias notes similarities between the emergence of feminism in the mid-1800s and its re-emergence 100 years later.

It is important to set any study of gender and politics in the context of the long history of the nineteenth- and early-twentieth-century women's rights movement because the second wave of feminism is in many ways cousin to the first. The earlier women's rights activists began their reform activities, as did their descendants in the 1960s, not as advocates for their own rights but as participants in campaigns to enhance the rights of others. Three such campaigns spawned the women's rights movement in the nineteenth century: temperance, anti-

Excerpted from *Faces of Feminism: An Activist's Reflections on the Women's Movement*, by Sheila Tobias (Boulder: Westview Press, 1997). Copyright © 1997 by Westview Press, a member of Perseus Books, L.L.C. Reprinted with permission.

48 • THE FEMINIST MOVEMENT

slavery, and social reform. From these movements, women emerged as competent reformers while experiencing frustration owing to their lack of power and influence in the parent movement—a similar experience, as I chronicle, to that of the women in the civil rights and anti-Vietnam War movements of the 1960s.

The nineteenth-century pioneers, much as twentieth-century second-wave feminists, were "radicalized" by their frustration. Lack of status, respect, and power drove them toward the position abolitionist Angelina Grimké expressed in 1838 when she said (speaking for all the women in her movement) that she could not make the contribution she was capable of making toward the emancipation of the Negro slave until and unless she achieved her own emancipation. The problem was partly male unwillingness to share a podium with a woman speaker—even one as powerful and energizing as Angelina Grimké is reported to have been—and partly a result of women's restricted participation in the male-dominated worlds of politics and the law.

In nineteenth-century America, even "free" white women (as opposed to slaves and Native American women) inhabited a subcitizen's class. According to common law, a married woman did not have property rights, which meant she could not own her own farm, have her own bank account, or do business as an independent contractor. Even the property she might inherit from her father or the income she earned if she worked outside the home did not legally belong to her but was, much as were her children, the property of the man she married. These indignities might have been addressed in the political arena had American women enjoyed legal, political, or even civil rights, but just as women were not empowered by property, so they were not empowered by the Constitution. Women could not sue in court, serve on juries, vote, or run for office. Legally, they could not even keep their own names once they married. The present-day tradition—now no longer legally required—of a female giving up her name upon marriage is a vestige of these long-standing limitations.

LIMITED LEGAL RIGHTS

In the family, thought to be the province of women, rights were restricted, too. A mother's right to custody of her children took second place to that of her children's father, and even though abortion in the early years of the nineteenth century was not prohibited by law, the decision to terminate a pregnancy belonged to the male parent. The unborn child, like the wife herself, was his "property." According to American civil law, which was based on English common law, a wife's marital status made her wholly dependent on her spouse. Upon marriage, a male and female became "one"—and that "one" was male. In legal terms, a married woman was a *femme couverte,* French for "a covered woman." Enclosed by her husband, a wife had no legal identity apart from his, and lacking legal standing, she was denied many of the other privileges of civil life.

In fact, in mid–nineteenth-century America, a white woman was freer if she was not married, and the most privileged legal status was reserved for widows, who as *ex couverte* were allowed some degree of independence regarding property ownership but still no civil or political rights. This was theory. In fact, with some exceptions, a widow's property would normally pass from her husband's control to her son's.

Extending from these barriers were limitations on women's employment and professional rights. The only profession truly open to and welcoming of educated women in the nineteenth century was schoolteaching. (Midwives were, for the most part, self-educated.) Single women wanting to teach completed high school and then two years of teacher training in "normal college," after which they went into the classroom. It was, in fact, this artificially constructed labor force of women, underpaid and willing (because they could not do anything else legally), that gave America a public education system much sooner than most other countries.

Women's unequal status and power are not something one can blame on the founding fathers or any other villain in American history. The traditions were as old as Western civilization; British and later U.S. law had simply codified them.

But beginning in midcentury, some of this code began to change. Lobbied for by fathers eager to protect their daughters' right to the families' property, particularly when they were married to irresponsible husbands, the first of a series of Married Women's Property Acts was passed in New York State in 1848. These statutes permitted women who had personally inherited property from their families to own and dispose freely of that inheritance. The laws went far in protecting women, but they did not yet incorporate women's own earnings. Females who went to work outside the home still owed that income to their husbands, and it remained their husbands' so long as they were wed. It is important to note that the Married Women's Property Acts were not initiated by women themselves. Although there did exist a feminist awareness before midcentury, there was no organized women's movement. These acts were the gift of moneyed fathers seeking to preserve their families' property. Their daughters were powerless to lobby for any change in their own status.

THE ROOTS OF REFORM

So why, the political analyst must ask, did women in the middle of the nineteenth century suddenly begin to challenge their political powerlessness? The answer to this question lies in a combination of conditions and the work of some remarkable human beings. Most Americans have heard of Susan B. Anthony and Elizabeth Cady Stanton and perhaps of Lucy Stone and Lucretia Mott as well. The vision and leadership provided by these and other women, people of extraordinary intellect, energy, and confidence, partly explain the birth of a women's movement during this period. But how they met, what brought them together, and why, after decades of quiescence, these women dedicated themselves to women's rights are interesting examples of the intersection of time and circumstance in history. The answer is that all of them were already politically active before they became "feminists." Like Angelina Grimké, they cut their political teeth on other people's causes.

The first of the nineteenth-century movements from which

"We Want as Much"

Sojourner Truth, speech delivered to the annual meeting of the American Equal Rights Association, 1867.

There is a great stir about colored men getting their rights, but not a word about the colored women; and if colored men get their rights, and not colored women get theirs, there will be a bad time about it. . . . I am above eighty years old; it is about time for me to be going. But I suppose I am kept here because something remains for me to do; I suppose I am yet to help break the chain. I have done a great deal of work—as much as a man, but did not get so much pay. I used to work in the field and bind grain, keeping up with the cradler; but men never doing no more, got twice as much pay. So with the German women. They work in the field and do as much work, but do not get the

these leaders emerged was temperance ("prohibition" in a later era), the drive to criminalize the sale of alcohol. On the surface, temperance might not seem fertile ground for women's rights. Temperance was a "do-gooder" Christian movement, stubborn in its belief that liquor was associated with sin. Employers, too, were eager to stem the absenteeism caused by drink. But because married women lacked control over their own and their husbands' earnings and because alcohol then, as now, was known to contribute to domestic abuse, temperance appealed to wives and mothers as a means of curbing their husbands' spending. So much was temperance linked to women's interests that substantial and sometimes effective campaigning against women's suffrage lasted well into the twentieth century, paid for by the so-called liquor interests. Manufacturers of "bottled spirits," dealers, distributors, and owners of bars united in their determination to keep women from getting the vote, pay. We do as much, we eat as much, we want as much. I suppose I am about the only colored woman that goes about to speak for the rights of the colored woman, I want to keep the thing stirring, now that the ice is broken. What we want is a little money. You men know that you get as much again as women when you write, or for what you do. When we get our rights, we shall not have to come to you for money, for then we shall have money enough of our own. It is a good consolation to know that when we have got this we shall not be coming to you any more. You have been having our right for so long, that you think, like a slaveholder, that you own us. I know that it is hard for one who has held the reins for so long to give up; it cuts like a knife. It will feel all better when it closes up again.

Beverly Guy-Sheftall, ed., *Words of Fire: An Anthology of African-American Feminist Thought*. The New Press, New York: 1995, pp. 37–38.

fearful that they would vote to prohibit the manufacture and distribution of alcohol at the first opportunity.

Temperance was Susan B. Anthony's movement. But she and many of her cofounders of America's first women's rights movement were also active in opposing slavery. Antislavery attracted moralists, Northerners and Southerners who, knowing slavery firsthand, could expose it passionately in print and at meetings. Some of the most powerful speakers against slavery were southern women or women who had studied America's "peculiar institution," and, like the Grimké sisters and Harriet Beecher Stowe, author of *Uncle Tom's Cabin,* could discuss it with knowledge and with emotional force as well. Slavery contradicted America's Judeo-Christian heritage and spoke particularly to women's values and their instincts for taking care of the dispossessed. Eventually, women activists in antislavery would find themselves conflicted when, thirty years later, the Negro male would be given the rights of citizenship and suffrage that American women, white and Negro, were denied. But in the 1830s and 1840s, American and British antislavery societies welcomed and made good use of their women members.

The third source of women's activism in the nineteenth century was a reformist tradition, one that found response among privileged women for the downtrodden, the mentally ill, and the immigrant. Many of these activists did not become women's rightists; doing good was more satisfying than doing well. The next generation of reformers made social history: Florence Nightingale, founder of the nursing profession; Jane Addams, leader of the Settlement House movement; and Florence Kelley, labor organizer on behalf of working women. Like their sisters in temperance and antislavery, many of the women reformers of the earlier era discovered their lack of power and influence in the course of seeking money and support for their other work. Elizabeth Cady Stanton and Lucretia Mott provide us with a dramatic cameo of how women activists, struggling to be useful on behalf of other people's movements, finally dared to start their own.

THE CATALYST FOR CHANGE

Stanton and Mott were united by their abolitionism and by their association with Quakerism, which was more egalitarian as regards gender than any other religion of their time. Stanton grew up in one family of antislavery activists and married into another; Mott was a minister in a Quaker meeting. As the story goes, in 1840 the two women traveled as official U.S. delegates to the World Antislavery Conference in London and found themselves relegated to the nonvoting section of the meeting. They had been duly selected by the American Antislavery Society to attend the meeting in London, but because they were women, they were not allowed to sit with their delegation, to speak to the assemblage, or to vote on any of the resolutions. It is important to think back to that time. Traveling to an international meeting was exhilarating and exhausting; the issue of ending slavery was of paramount importance to our nation and to the world. The women had been laboring side by side with antislavery men for many years. They had earned their delegate status. But simply because they were women, such rights were denied them.

Think, too, of the contradictions. The movement that had begun in Britain as an effort to end the slave trade in the British colonies was dedicated to the elimination of slavery; yet politically, that same movement (or at least its English branch) was unwilling to fully credential its own female delegates. Not surprisingly, as the story continues, Stanton and Mott sat in the balcony for this weeks-long conference, fumed, and one day nudged each other and (may have) said, "The issue of slavery may be too important to be diverted by any other. But when this business is over, we must turn our attention to women's rights." The antislavery struggle, according to the editors of the *History of Woman Suffrage in America,* was "the single most important factor in creating the woman's rights movement in America."

MIRRORING THE PAST

There is a parallel in the story of the origins of the second wave of feminism in the 1960s. Student activists joined women's liberation groups because, however valiantly they fought alongside their "brothers" in the 1960s battles for civil rights and peace in Vietnam, "radical" men turned out to be traditional when it came to sharing power with radical women. As countless memoirs from the 1960s have documented, women in the various student movements were assigned to the mimeograph and coffee machines, while their menfolk planned and executed the "revolution." In caucuses and consciousness-raising, 1960s women no doubt echoed Stanton and Mott: "Civil rights and the war in Vietnam are too important to be diverted by the issue of our rights and status. But when this campaign is won, it will be our turn." And, indeed, when the anti–Vietnam War campaign came to a temporary halt in the aftermath of Richard Nixon's election in 1968, a movement for "women's liberation" began.

The Suffrage Movement's Lessons for Democracy

LUCINDA DESHA ROBB

Lucinda Desha Robb works at the National Archives, where she is project director for *Our Mothers Before Us: Women in Democracy, 1789–1920.* In the following piece, she argues that the suffrage movement changed much more than merely the U.S. Constitution. During the movement, she notes, women were divided on whether they wanted the right to vote. The long, protracted public debate between suffragists and antisuffragists, which included developing grassroots organizations, campaigning, writing letters to politicians and newspapers, and marshaling reasons and defending one's position, constitutes the essence of democratic activity, according to Robb. As she sees it, this was political activity through which women learned the potential and importance of democratic participation, refined their political credentials, and challenged assumptions about their political capacities.

It is tempting to hypothesize that women are more uniform and monolithic in their opinions than they really are. Much of the difficulty in trying to define a "women's political agenda" comes from the fact that women can be located all over the political map. This idea was brought home to me when I started reading through the petitions and letters opposing woman suffrage. While huge numbers of women worked to get the vote, a significant number of women not only opposed suffrage but worked actively to defeat it.

It startled me to learn that these antisuffrage women were

Excerpted from "Lessons from the Women's Suffrage Movement," by Lucinda Desha Robb, *A Voice of Our Own: Leading American Women Celebrate the Right to Vote*, edited by Nancy Neuman. Copyright © 1996 by Jossey-Bass Publishers, Inc. Reprinted by permission of Jossey-Bass, Inc., a subsidiary of John Wiley & Sons, Inc.

not self-loathing troglodyte [primitive or outmoded] puppets. While many of the women who worked against suffrage were upper-class socially prominent "conservative" women (none of which makes their opinions any less valid), some of these same antisuffrage women were also challenging the status quo and creating new roles for women. The antisuffrage ranks included the celebrated muckraker and Standard Oil nemesis Ida Tarbell, women's education advocate Catherine Beecher, and prison and insane asylum reformer Dorothea Dix. Union organizer "Mother" Jones thought the struggle for suffrage was a waste of time that kept women from focusing on the real issues of economics. The first woman lawyer, Phoebe Couzins, started out working for woman suffrage and then, to the enormous dismay of Susan B. Anthony and others, changed her mind and came out against it! Even the venerable Lucretia Coffin Mott, one of the Founding Mothers of the women's rights movement, originally had doubts about the wisdom of seeking the vote.

THE SPECIAL ROLE OF WOMEN

Arguments set forth by the Massachusetts Association Opposed to the Further Extension of Suffrage to Women are representative of the feelings of many antisuffragists. Along traditional lines, the association argued that the most important influence a woman can have is as a wife and mother. Not having a very high opinion of the political process, the association's members also did not want to be corrupted by it, as they thought women surely would be if they became politically involved.

Like the suffragists, however, many antisuffragists took great pride in the accomplishments of women and lauded their work as reformers. To them, the limitation of women's political activity was not a constraint; it was a virtue that allowed women to advise both political parties on a nonpartisan basis. In short, they felt that women would have a chance to make the world a better place if they worked within their own separate sphere.

As support for woman suffrage increased so did the rancor

between the suffrage and antisuffrage women, each group un-
fathomable to and intolerant of the other. Women on both
sides of the issue accused their opponents of not being "real"
women. Suffragists ridiculed antisuffragists as "useless parasites"
and "a disgrace to their sex." The antisuffragists, horrified at
militant suffragists picketing outside the White House while
the country was at war, declared that woman suffrage would
"be an endorsement of nagging as a national policy." Naturally
each camp claimed to represent the majority of women.

Ironically the antisuffragists' effort to stay out of politics effectively politicized them, which helped reconcile them to
woman suffrage when it finally passed. After all, once you have
learned to debate, make speeches, lobby, campaign, fundraise,
and organize on an issue, voting every two years doesn't seem
so earth-shattering.

Today, while it would be easy enough to find a woman who
did not vote in the last election, it would be difficult to find
one who thought she should not have the right to vote. New
issues have come to the forefront of the political debate, but
they are just as hotly contested among women as suffrage was
earlier. The history of women's political activism includes both
the Phyllis Schlaflys [a prominent, conservative antifeminist]
and the Gloria Steinems [a prominent, liberal feminist]. As far
as I can tell, just about the only thing that the majority of
women seemed to believe in during the era of the woman
suffrage movement was that women are superior to men. I
don't know if *that* belief has changed all that much. . . .

THE EFFECT OF WOMEN VOTING

The first election after women gained the right to vote was no
big deal. I don't mean to imply that it wasn't enormously important to those women who had helped make suffrage a reality. It was just that, for the most part, things went on as normal. Women had the vote, but they didn't seem to vote all that
differently from men. If the antisuffragists' dire predictions
about soaring divorce rates didn't come true, neither did the
suffragists' dreams of a utopian society. After a few years passed,

people couldn't seem to remember what the fuss was all about. Why didn't something more noteworthy happen?

Part of the reason no marked change occurred is that although suffrage was official recognition of women's political participation, women had been influencing and making changes in American democracy all along. Long before the 19th Amendment was ratified, the 1st Amendment had given women the right to freedom of speech and of the press, the right to peaceably assemble, and the right to petition the government for a redress of grievances. So women debated and spoke in public, testified before congressional committees, and addressed state legislatures. In the early days of the suffrage movement, when no woman was allowed to stay in the "better" hotels unaccompanied by a man, Susan B. Anthony traveled all over the country and scandalized people by speaking to audiences of both men and women.

Later on, when the ranks of women working for suffrage swelled and public speaking for women became more acceptable, suffragists learned to drive their motorcars up to street corners and talk into empty space until a crowd formed. They were taught how to defuse hecklers and win the crowds to their cause with humor. As suffragist Maud Malone was speaking to a New York City crowd, a hostile male voice from the crowd interrupted her. "How'd you like to be a man?" the heckler sneered. "Not much," she replied. "How would you?"

GRASSROOTS ORGANIZATIONS AND ACTIVITIES

Women became adept at grassroots organization. The staid traditional and hierarchical National American Woman Suffrage Association believed that the way to win the vote was by careful persuasion, lobbying, and the building up of relationships—a slow but inevitable process by which it helped make woman suffrage acceptable to the general public. Schools were set up for suffragists where they learned how to canvass their neighborhoods, set up suffrage clubs, and lobby local politicians.

Women's organizations such as the General Federation of

Suffrage Alleviates Oppression

"Hear me patiently," the woman on the platform coaxed her audience, as she recounted chilling stories of brutalized women whose children were wrongfully taken from them. Moments later, her voice rising, she exulted in the courage and accomplishments of other women: reformers, artists, and entrepreneurs who dared to step outside the sphere assigned to them. Then she broke into a familiar ballad, known for its heartrending description of the seamstress's life. Her voice quavered as she sang:

Stitch, stitch, stitch!
In poverty, hunger and dirt
Sewing at once with a double thread
A shroud as well as a shirt.

The audience shifted in their seats, a few dabbed at their

Women's Clubs and the National Congress of Mothers formed special committees to track the political activities of their local, state, and national representatives. These committees interviewed prospective political candidates about their positions on issues and placed women in the galleries in capitols around the country to take careful notice of how their legislators voted.

Women wrote letters to their congressmen and editors, published columns in national newspapers, and made their living as professional reporters. When that wasn't enough, they published their own newspapers and other informational materials, complete with facts and statistics compiled through their own research.

THE CHANGING ROLE OF WOMEN

The roles that women could play within government were changing as well. In the late 1800s, they made job inroads as eyes; some stared at the woman's shortened skirt and trousers, which they had forgotten about as she spoke. She closed her eyes with a powerful call to the people there to join her in working for reform, pleading with them to support temperance laws and woman's right to vote: "For woman to vote then, is to elevate her in the scale of humanity.... And her elevation will carry with it the elevation and well being of the race. So we believe, and so we pray, God speed the day of woman's enfranchisement!" The audience applauded passionately. Many lingered after the speech was over. Some invited the woman to speak in their own small towns. Others, anticipating her sympathetic response, sought to share a fearsome confidence.

Anne C. Coon, ed., *Hear Me Patiently: The Reform Speeches of Amelia Jenks Bloomer.* Westport, CT: Greenwood Press, 1994, p. 1.

civil servants, inspectors, judges, clerks, and public administrators. As lawyers, they argued cases in front of the Supreme Court, where they were admitted to practice in 1879.

Long before they could vote nationwide, women ran for the presidency of the United States (most notably Victoria Woodhull in 1872 and Belva Lockwood in 1884). They served as mayors, city councilwomen, school board representatives, and members of state legislatures. The voters of Oskaloosa, Kansas, elected the first all-female city government in 1888, as a protest against the mismanagement of the previous city council. The new city council enforced the laws, made several civic improvements, and brought the treasury from a debt to a surplus. The women were reelected the following year.

As not the least of these activities, in a time before CNN and public opinion polls, women collected tens of millions of signatures for hundreds of thousands of petitions supporting the legislation they believed in. In 1917, New York women collected over a million signatures on a petition to the state legislature from women seeking suffrage. To forestall accusations that they had inflated the number of signatures, the women put all the signature sheets on placards and marched, two and four abreast, in a procession that covered over half a mile. In the course of such ever growing political activity, women managed slowly to change the standards that dictated what women were allowed to do.

How Much Was Changed

Although Susan B. Anthony did not live to see ratification of the amendment that was named for her, she was aware of the changes she and others had accomplished in their lifetimes, and she felt confident that women eventually would carry the day. This letter from Anthony to her great friend Elizabeth Cady Stanton, written days before Stanton's death in 1902, is reprinted in *The History of Woman Suffrage*.

> We little dreamed when we began this contest, optimistic with the hope and buoyancy of youth, that half a century later we would be compelled to leave the finish of the battle to another generation of women. But our hearts are filled with joy to know that they enter upon this task equipped with a college education, with business experience, with the fully admitted right to speak in public—all of which were denied to women fifty years ago. They have practically but one point to gain—the suffrage: we had all. These strong, courageous, capable young women will take our place and complete our work. There is an army of them where we were but a handful. Ancient prejudice has become so softened, public sentiment so liberalized and women have so thoroughly demonstrated their ability to leave not a shadow of doubt that they will carry our cause to victory.

As odd as it may sound, one of the most important lessons of the woman suffrage movement may be the relative unimportance of suffrage all by itself. Around election time, television commentators talk about how few eligible voters actually vote. Celebrities and nonprofit groups produce eye-catching public service announcements to convince us to participate in this most minimal requirement of democracy. But voting is something we do at most once a year, and by itself, it is not always the best way to communicate with Washington.

The messages we voters send can be very confusing. Politicians cannot read our minds, and polling is a notoriously unreliable way of ascertaining just how strongly people care about an issue. Technically we are a repúblic, not a democracy. When we vote, we authorize someone else to make myriad decisions for us so that we don't have to spend all our own time thinking about the gross domestic product and dairy regulation and U.S. political interests in Burkina Faso. But many rights other than the vote are guaranteed by the Constitution, rights that we are able to—and need to—take advantage of if we want to influence our government more directly. Democracy requires a lot of day-to-day maintenance; going to school board meetings is much more effective than just complaining about the educational system.

The struggle for woman suffrage is traditionally believed to have started in 1848, when the right to vote was included among the resolutions passed at the Seneca Falls women's rights convention. Only one of the original signers at the convention, a young glove maker named Charlotte Woodward, would live to see the 19th Amendment ratified seventy-two years later. It is not surprising that one of the constant frustrations of suffrage organizers was how long the struggle was taking. But perhaps the long wait was not such a terrible thing. The years of hard work women put into making suffrage a reality taught them the full potential of democracy and how to employ that potential. They learned grassroots skills and gained the political credentials that made them more effective and laid the groundwork for their increasing participation in government. After all, the vote alone should never be the goal; the goal is what you can do with the vote.

Taking a New Look at the Woman Suffrage Movement

Robert Cooney

The author of this selection, Robert Cooney, works for the National Women's History Project, a nonprofit organization that provides educational material recognizing the historic accomplishments of women. Cooney contends that the historic importance of the suffrage movement is neglected by most historians and by the American public generally. As Cooney sees it, the struggle for the right to vote was fought by true heroes, by women and men of courage, integrity, and perseverance. He points out that the long campaign for suffrage was marked by idealism, sacrifice, and high drama, and that it ultimately won the most basic political right for half of American citizens. Consequently, Cooney believes, the names of those who led the suffrage movement should rank among the most famous names in American history. Cooney suggests that perhaps one reason the suffrage movement has often been ignored is because it achieved its goals without any bloodshed. For Cooney, however, this is only more reason to praise the movement's leaders.

W omen vote today because of the woman's suffrage movement, a courageous and persistent political campaign which lasted over 72 years, involved tens of thousands of women and men, and resulted in enfranchising one-half of the citizens of the United States.

Inspired by idealism and grounded in sacrifice, the suffrage campaign is of enormous political and social significance yet it is virtually unacknowledged in the chronicles of American history.

Had the suffrage movement not been so ignored by historians, women like Lucretia Mott, Carrie Chapman Catt and Alice Paul would be as familiar to most Americans as Thomas Jefferson, Theodore Roosevelt or Martin Luther King, Jr.

We would know the story of how women were denied the right to vote despite the lofty words of the Constitution, how women were betrayed after the Civil War, defeated and often cheated in election after election, and how they were forced to fight for their rights against entrenched opposition with virtually no financial, legal or political power.

If the history of the suffrage movement was better known, we would understand that democracy for the first 150 years in America included half of the population. And we would realize that this situation changed only after the enormous efforts of American citizens in what remains one of the most remarkable and successful nonviolent efforts to change ingrained social attitudes and institutions in the modern era.

A Dramatic Victory

For women won the vote. They were not given it, granted it, or anything else. They won it as truly as any political campaign is ultimately won or lost. And they won it, repeatedly, by the slimmest of margins, which only underscores the difficulty and magnitude of their victories.

In the successful California referendum of 1911, the margin was one vote per precinct! In the House, suffrage passed the first time by exactly the number needed with supporters coming in from the hospital and funeral home to cast their ballots. In the Senate it passed by two votes. The ratification in Tennessee, the last state, passed the legislature in 1920 by a single vote, at the very last minute, during a recount.

Women were a poor, unarmed and disenfranchised class when they first organized to gain political power in the mid-1800s. The struggle for the ballot took over 70 years of constant, determined campaigning, yet it didn't take a single life, and its achievement has lasted.

Compare this with male-led independence movements. Without firing a shot, throwing a rock, or issuing a personal threat, women won for themselves rights that men have launched violent rebellions to achieve. This deliberate rejection of violence may be one of the reasons the movement has not received the attention lavished on other, bloody periods of American history—or on the suffrage movement in Britain.

But it should not deceive us; this struggle was waged every bit as seriously as any struggle for equality, and we would do well to consider how women were able to do what men have rarely even tried, changing society in a positive and lasting way without violence and death.

The movement's many nonviolent strategies deserve closer inspection particularly because they repeatedly offered suffragists the way out of strategic binds, dead ends, discouragements and immobility.

The nonviolent approach was a logical strategy as a remarkable number of prominent suffrage leaders, from Lucretia Mott to Alice Paul, were Quakers and pacifists, exponents of nonresistance and opponents of war and violence. They were clear about their goals: not victory over men, but equality; not constant war, but reconciliation.

THE WOMEN WHO WON

Like the now-celebrated civil rights movement, women suffrage records the recent and useful experiences of ordinary citizens forced to fight for their own rights against tremendous odds and social inequities.

Here are models of political leadership, of women organizers and administrators, activists and lobbyists. Here are the first women lawyers and doctors and ministers, the first women candidates, the first office-holders. Here are stories of achievement, of ingenious strategies and outrageous tactics used to outwit the opponents and make the most of limited resources. Here are new definitions and images of women in our national life which give a more accurate picture of the past and which help explain the way American women are treated today.

The suffrage movement included many Americans whose talents and abilities would have made them prime candidates for national office had the political system, and their opportunities been equal.

Women like Elizabeth Cady Stanton, Susan B. Anthony, Lucy Stone, Frances Willard, Jane Addams, Louise Bowen, Ida W. Wells-Barnett, Carrie Chapman Catt, Mary Church Terrell, Alice Paul and others proved themselves, even without the franchise, to be politically competent, highly influential and widely respected leaders with few equals among their male contemporaries.

The suffrage movement offers a unique window onto the emergence of women into American political life. This is where many of the intelligent, active, politically oriented women of the time, denied the right to participate directly in national politics, went. They put their energy into attacking social problems directly and organizing among themselves, locally and nationally, for their own rights.

A POPULAR MISCONCEPTION

Yet despite all of this, the suffrage movement has been routinely and consistently ignored, and when it has not been ignored it has been substantially misrepresented. The result is the misconception today—when there is any conception at all— of the suffrage movement as being essentially an old, passive, white, upper-class, naive, inconsequential cause, one hardly worthy of attention much less respect. It is treated as a lone curiosity with nothing to teach us, or worse, as a target for clever academics to critique. Fortunately, there are some notable exceptions, but this attitude and the lack of accurate information available lie at the heart of the problem.

A new look at the American woman suffrage movement reveals an entity far different from any popular conception. Not a dour, old-woman cause benevolently recognized by Congressional gods, but a movement of female organizers, leaders, politicians, journalists, visionaries, rabble rousers, and warriors.

It was an active, controversial, multi-faceted, challenging, passionate movement of the best and brightest women in America, from all backgrounds, who, in modern parlance, boldly went where no woman had ever gone before.

But rather than acknowledging this, and recognizing that women had to fight for their rights because for the first 150 years American "democracy" actually included half of the population, many academics and historians have chosen to ignore, discount, marginalize, ridicule and/or dismiss the entire 72-year, nationwide, "successful" suffrage movement.

CENSORING THE STORY

In many history textbooks, the entire movement is summed up in one sentence: "In 1920, Congress gave women the right to vote."

Eleanor Flexner noted this censorship in her landmark book *Century of Struggle: The Woman's Rights Movement in the United States,* and quoted the late historian Arthur Schlesinger chiding his colleagues back in 1928 for neglecting women. Schlesinger wrote:

> An examination of the standard histories of the United States and of the history textbooks in use in our schools raises the pertinent question whether women have ever made any contributions to American national progress that are worthy of record. If the silence of the historians is to mean anything, it would appear that one-half of our population have been negligible factors in our country's history . . . any consideration of woman's part in American history must include the protracted struggle of the sex for larger rights and opportunities, a story that is in itself one of the noblest chapters in the history of American democracy.

After Schlesinger wrote this, the civil rights movement added another "noble chapter" to American history, and helped create a new context and vocabulary with which to analyze earlier movements for social change.

The suffrage movement stands as a lasting affirmation of

our country's democratic promise for it re-emphasizes the importance of the most fundamental democratic value, the right to vote. Flexner wrote of this in 1975:

> Recently there has been a tendency to low-rate the winning of woman suffrage as something less than the great achievement it seemed to those who carried on the struggle. . . . Yet full political citizenship was, for women as for any other group arbitrarily deprived of it, a vital step toward winning full human dignity and the recognition that women, too, are endowed with the faculty of reason, the power of judgment, the capacity for social responsibility and effective action. As a matter of fact, the opposition to woman suffrage itself bears witness, in a perverse kind of way, to its significance; nothing unimportant would have been so bitterly resisted. If one thinks of those, white and black, who laid down their lives only a few years ago in order that southern black men and women could register to vote, and then actually "vote," it seems clear that their efforts and sacrifices were no idle exercise in gallantry and that, without the vote, no social or legal reform was either possible, or lasting.

> The achievement of the vote for women was extraordinarily difficult, infinitely more so than most people realize, since those who ought to have included it in the history of this country simply obliterated the whole story.

A Forgotten Story

So completely and so quickly was the story lost that it was virtually unknown to the next generation. Suffrage leader Gertrude Foster Brown tells of interviewing one of the women who persuaded the Illinois legislature to grant presidential suffrage in 1913, a key breakthrough in the struggle for national suffrage. She ends her article with this anecdote:

> As I sat with Mrs. Booth and her husband some years ago and they told me the tale of the winning of Illinois, he,

strangely enough, remembering better than she the details of the long struggle, it was the listening young people who marked for us how far the world has moved since then. Their son and daughter, then grown, sat round-eyed and enthralled by the story. They had never heard it. Did women, just because they were women, ever have to fight against such incredible odds? And was it their mother who had played the leading role on such a stage? Like most young people they had always taken her for granted—retiring, thoughtful, quiet and kind, just a mighty nice mother—and suddenly they saw her a general, a heroine in one of the great dramas of the world. For this Illinois victory was the turning point in the enfranchisement of twenty-five millions of women.

THE LARGER STORY IS DEMOCRACY

You need not be a feminist, female, or even political to enjoy learning about the suffrage movement. For while the subject is woman suffrage, the larger story is about democracy, and how a powerless class in America won concessions and guarantees from those in power without threatening them with violence or death. We approach this topic not as women or men but as students of American history. We see the woman suffrage movement as a topic of its own, worthy of study and rich with content, apart from the whole field of women's history, notable women, women of achievement, feminist theory or other more general topics where it has previously resided.

Men were suffragists. The suffrage movement both included men as supporters and depended on men for their votes. Even when state measures were lost, the suffrage question often received tens of thousands of male votes of approval, and ultimately, a virtually all-male Senate and House had to approve the amendment, along with 36 virtually all-male state legislatures. Courageous men risked ridicule and worse to actively support women's rights, and they offer far better role models today than many better-known political and military figures.

The suffrage movement also offers us a new cultural heritage, covering not only historical figures and events, but extraordinary personalities, intense relationships, colorful experiences and legendary exploits. Students will find a new view of American history, fuller and richer with new heroes. Next to George Washington and his cherry tree we can set young Carrie Chapman Catt driving a wagon across the prairie by "dead reckoning" or brave Lucretia Mott trusting her own safety to a member of the mob roused against her. We can honor Sojourner Truth [an early African American feminist] no less than Patrick Henry, and Alice Paul no less than Woodrow Wilson.

THE LEGACY OF THE MOVEMENT

The suffrage movement holds a particular relevance now as it has helped lead us as a country and a people to where we are today. It celebrates rights won and honors those who helped win them. It is both an example of history suppressed and misunderstood and a lesson of history triumphant. It puts women back into our national history as participants. It reminds us of the necessity of progressive leaders, organizers, and visionaries in every local community.

It is the origin of the yet-unpassed Equal Rights Amendment. It exposed the misplaced fears and prejudices of anti-suffragists, and offers a sobering reminder that too many of these same foolish, reactionary attitudes of 100 years ago still exist today. Clearly the wider goal of women's true equality and freedom has not yet been achieved, but the victorious woman suffrage movement offers a new generation of activists a solid base on which to build the future.

Harriot Stanton Blatch summarized the movement's legacy best when she wrote: "Perhaps some day men will raise a tablet reading in letters of gold: 'All honor to women, the first disenfranchised class in history who unaided by any political party won enfranchisement by its own effort alone, and achieved the victory without the shedding of a drop of human blood. All the honor to the women of the world!'"

CHAPTER 2

THE PERSONAL IS POLITICAL: FEMINISM'S SECOND WAVE

AMERICAN
SOCIAL
MOVEMENTS

The Birth Control Movement

JAMES REED

In this selection, James Reed, a professor of history at Rutgers University, discusses the development of the birth control movement in the early decades of the twentieth century. In Reed's account, the central figure of that movement was Margaret Sanger, who succeeded in removing the negative stigma attached to contraception by dramatizing the plight of working-class women in America. Before birth control was widely available, Reed notes, it was often the case that a woman's health and hopes for a better life were destroyed by unwanted pregnancies. According to Reed, Sanger believed that access to contraception was of the highest importance for the liberation and self-determination of women. Although Sanger is most known for her campaign for birth control, Reed argues, this effort was motivated by a deep commitment to feminism in general.

M argaret Sanger (1879–1966) led a successful campaign from 1914 to 1937 to remove the stigma of obscenity from contraception and to establish a nationwide system of clinics where women could obtain reliable birth control services. She organized research, recruited manufacturers for birth control devices, and won court battles that modified the Comstock laws [1873 laws prohibiting the distribution of obscenities, which included birth control devices and information about them] and laid the groundwork for the formal acceptance of birth control by organized medicine in 1937. After World War II she played key roles in the rise of an international planned parenthood movement and in the development of the birth control pill. Through these achievements she had a greater impact on the world than any other American woman. In 1909, however, she was a thirty-year-old suburban housewife, raising three children in Hastings-on-Hudson, and waiting for her husband to return home from the nine-to-five grind in the city.

Sanger was drawn into her career as a reformer through a series of vivid personal experiences. "World hunger" and dissatisfaction with life in suburbia drew her to the rebel's paradise of pre–World War I New York. There she sought personal freedom and discovered the plight of the city's poor women. Most important, she found ideas that connected her problems with those of other women and justified rebellion against the father and husband who had dominated her life and whom she blamed for isolating her from the world of experience beyond the home.

SANGER'S STRATEGY AND SUCCESS

Through her public career she realized a personal desire for self-fulfillment free from the burdens imposed on her as a daughter, wife, and mother, but she owed the tremendous success she enjoyed as a reformer to an ability to explain her cause in terms that the general public could understand and accept. Her triumphs symbolized a growing awareness among thousands of Americans that the maintenance of stable families depended on more satisfactory sexual adjustment. Birth control might provide a means of reconciling marital passion with the desire for fewer children, a higher standard of living, and greater personal freedom, but many Americans feared that the easy separation of sex from procreation would undermine public morality and weaken the family. Sanger became the dominant figure in the history of contraception by providing social justification for practices that had once seemed wholly personal and selfish. By dramatizing the suffering of working-class women whose health and hopes for a better life were destroyed by unwanted pregnancies, she forced public recognition of what was already a fact of middle-class behavior. The horrible specter she raised of rampant abortion, high maternal mortality, and the instability of family life among the impoverished helped to define by contrast the strengths of middle-class family life.

The clinics necessary to provide contraceptive services to indigent women also served as centers of education where private practitioners were instructed in contraceptive technique, a subject not taught in medical schools. The thousands of club women who rallied behind Sanger's banner not only helped to free lower-class women from fear of pregnancy but also freed themselves by bringing their own conduct into the open and by providing the means through which doctors in private practice could learn about birth control. Although she drew most of her support from among the privileged, Sanger would have passionately resented any attempt to link her with efforts to preserve the domestic status quo. She hoped that women in control of themselves would become a revolutionary force by choosing to rear children only under the best possible conditions, thereby eliminating not only poverty but mediocrity as well.

CRITICAL VOICES

The Roman Catholics and medical men who were the most vehement critics of Sanger's utopian vision argued that she had nothing new to offer. Birth controllers, they said, were simply trying to promote dangerous practices that had been discredited and suppressed in the nineteenth century. Sanger's critics were right when they noted that she had no new technology to offer, but their persistent hostility had little to do with the effectiveness and safety of birth control methods. Vaginal diaphragms, cervical caps, spermicidal compounds, condoms, and a safe period were all known in the nineteenth century. Yet before Sanger no one undertook the systematic evaluation of birth control methods to separate the safe and effective from the unreliable and dangerous. Attitudes toward sex, women, and the family, rather than lack of technical know-how, account for most of the hostility toward birth control. Once birth controllers convinced the public that the separation of sex from procreation was morally safe, if not socially essential, then the limitations of existing birth control methods would be a minor inconvenience rather than a major obstacle to the acceptance of birth control by organized medicine and by government.

Sanger began her reform career as one of many individuals demanding wholesale social change in an era of reform. Her willingness to concentrate on one issue and her changing tactics alienated old comrades. She understood, however, that the fight for acceptance of birth control depended on manipulation of public opinion, victories in court, and skillful lobbying among professional elites. Each audience required a different strategy of change. Thus, she had to disassociate herself from the radicals and medical heretics who were the first to advocate family limitation. She retained many assumptions and attitudes drawn from earlier reformers, but her burning conviction that birth control was *the* most important concrete step that could be taken to improve the quality of life sprang from her own experience as a daughter, wife, nurse, and radical agitator....

BANNED WRITINGS

By 1912, while continuing to work as a nurse, she had established herself as a writer and speaker in socialist circles. The scandal of prostitution, the ravages of venereal disease, and their common source in the wage system were popular themes in socialist literature. As a nurse, she often spoke to working women's groups on sexual hygiene. Beginning in November 1912, *The Call,* New York's socialist daily, published a series of her Sunday supplement articles on female sexuality. The series ran until February 9, 1913, when the Post Office ruled that an article on syphilis was unmailable under the Comstock Act.

If women could not read the plain truth about venereal disease, a recognized social evil, then they certainly would never be allowed knowledge of contraception, an essential in any practical plan of liberation. Emma Goldman had advocated family limitation since her experience of nursing among Manhattan's poor in the 1890s. Her exploits were legend among cultural rebels, but birth control was a minor feature of Goldman's revolutionary platform. Infuriated by censorship of her *Call* articles, Sanger turned the reluctance of doctors to provide contraceptive information into a symbol of oppression and thus defined a cause for her own.

During her student nursing days Sanger had been called out on maternity cases. Sometimes the doctor did not arrive in time, and the nurse had to assist the delivery. The close relationship with the patient created by shared experience was rewarding. Mutual confidence sometimes gave the patient courage to ask a question she feared to put to a man. "Miss Higgins, what should I do not to have another baby right away?" When the nurse asked the doctor, the usual answer was, "She ought to be ashamed of herself to talk to a young girl about things like that."

DIRE CONDITIONS FOR THE POOR

In 1912, Sanger was not "a young girl" but a mother of three who knew that the middle classes used condoms and withdrawal. Many of her patients were poor. Sex was one of the few luxuries their husbands had, and these men refused to limit their own enjoyment. Too many children meant crowding, lack of proper nurture, and a vicious cycle of poverty spawned by the ignorance and helplessness of women. The Lower East Side of Manhattan seemed like a hell where the wretched "were beyond the scope of organized charity or religion." Pregnancy was a chronic condition among the women of this district. On Saturday nights Sanger saw lines of fifty to one hundred women who stood "with their shawls over their heads waiting outside the office of the five-dollar abortionist." Constantly the nurse heard pleas for the "secret rich people have" to stop the babies from coming and "the story told a thousand times of death from abortion and children going into institutions."

Both Sanger and Goldman witnessed deaths from induced abortions. A 1917 study by a physician of 464 indigent women who received care in the dispensaries of New York's Department of Health revealed the stark reality of the frequency of resort to abortion among the poor. Of the 192 of

Right to Privacy and Birth Control

United States Supreme Court, Eisenstadt v. Baird, *405 U.S. 438 (1972).*

If under *Griswold* [the Supreme Court decision that made contraceptives legal for married couples] the distribution of contraceptives to married persons cannot be prohibited, a ban on distribution to unmarried persons would be equally impermissible. It is true that in *Griswold* the right of privacy in question inhered in the marital relationship. Yet the marital couple is not an independent entity with a mind and heart of its own, but an association of two individuals each with a separate intellectual and emotional makeup. If the right of privacy means anything, it is the right of the individual, married or single, to be free from unwarranted governmental intrusion into matters so fundamentally affecting a person as the decision whether to bear or beget a child.

http://laws.findlaw.com/us/405/438.html.

these women who never used contraceptives, 104 had a history of abortions. There were 202 abortions, or an average of almost two apiece.

Sanger claimed that the death of one of her patients from a second self-induced abortion was the traumatic event that made her a "Woman Rebel." Sadie Sachs was the wife of a truck driver and the mother of three small children. Her tiny apartment reflected industry and desire to raise her family properly despite slum conditions. Called in to nurse Mrs. Sachs through an infection following a self-induced abortion, Sanger spent three weeks of backbreaking work in the heat of a tenement where every drop of water had to be carried up three flights of stairs. Mrs. Sachs lived to beg to be told how to prevent another pregnancy. The doctor was "a kindly man ... but such incidents had become so familiar to him that he had long since lost whatever delicacy he might once have had." "Tell Jake to sleep on the roof."

A Tragic Death

Several months later Sanger was called back to the Sachs apartment to find Sadie in a coma following another abortion. For Sanger her death symbolized the blindness of father, husband, male doctors, and fellow radicals to the needs of women. She resolved never "to go back to merely keeping alive" and to do something to change "the destiny of mothers whose miseries were as vast as the sky."

Sanger used the Sachs story with great effect in her campaigns for birth control. One historian has suggested that the story represents "a common autobiographical ploy of reformers," a self-justifying myth that often obscures complex motivation. Whether or not Sadie Sachs actually existed, or her story represented a composite of several experiences, some of them perhaps borrowed from other nurses, is beyond proof. The abortion problem was real, and Sanger's portrayal of the attitude of physicians toward contraception was accurate, although there were a few doctors who argued that the poor wanted and could effectively use contraceptive information. Sanger's intense reaction to the abortion problem sprang, in part, from her belief that many of her contemporaries, although sympathetic toward the poor, were indifferent to the special plight of women. Her description of tenement life contrasts with the picture drawn by the journalist Hutchins Hapgood in *Spirit of the Ghetto* (1902). Hapgood described a colorful, aspiring, and self-reliant people on the way up, whose rich culture and religious values not only made tenement life endurable but reflected a redeeming sense of community lacking in American culture. He made no mention of lines of women queued up in front of abortion mills.

On the Lower East Side both hope and social mobility were realities, as were defeat and despair. But the contrast between the Sanger and the Hapgood visions of life in the Jewish ghetto helps to explain the uncompromising resentment Sanger felt toward other reformers who were less concerned about the plight of women. Thirty-four and the tubercular mother of three, Sanger's feeling of having been trapped by marriage made the suffering of tenement mothers her own. There seemed to be no justice for these women, whose "weary misshapen bodies, always ailing, never failing, were destined to be thrown on the scrap heap before they were thirty-five." Neither the radical nor liberal imagination envisioned a basically different situation for women. A distinctively female voice was needed. Women "had to be made aware of how they were being shackled, and roused to mutiny."

BIRTH CONTROL FOR WOMEN

Raising the female consciousness of working women would only lead to frustration, Sanger believed, unless effective contraceptive means were available. She decided that her first task was to find an effective birth control method that depended entirely on the woman. Douching, spermicidal mixtures, tampons, and cervical caps all found advocates in the nineteenth century, but these methods had never been studied systematically, and even middle-class women had great difficulty in obtaining reliable contraceptive information. Better information on contraception could be obtained from an anarchist leaflet than from a medical journal. . . .

Sanger returned from Europe in early 1914 armed with French pessaries, formulas for suppositories and douches, and new determination to defy the Comstock laws. Her first task, she believed, was to raise the consciousness of working women so that they would support her demand for free dissemination of birth control information. In March 1914 she published the first issue of *The Woman Rebel,* with the old anarchist slogan "No God, No Masters!" tacked to the mast. Subscribers recruited through labor union lists and notices in radical journals heard in eight issues of the degradation of labor through over-production of children. The *Rebel* bitterly denounced "the diseased, perverted, hypocritical ghouls of American civilization," "the Baptist Church and its allies, those 'Christian Associations,' that are subsidized by the Rockefellers and other criminals in order to kill the spirit of the workers of America." Readers were exhorted to remember Ludlow, the Colorado strike against Standard Oil during which thirteen members of strikers' families were killed by state militia. "Remember the men and women and children who were sacrificed in order that John D. Rockefeller, Jr. might continue his noble career of charity and philanthropy as a supporter of the Christian faith."

Max Eastman, editor of *The Masses,* found Sanger's "over-conscious extremism" irritating and complained that "the Woman Rebel seems to give a little more strength to the business of shocking the Bourgeoisie than the Bourgeoisie are really worth." Emma Goldman, however, approved the *Rebel's* tone; the journal sold splendidly at anarchist lectures, "as the subject you are treating is really the main thing people are interested in. Not one of my lectures brings out such a crowd as the one on the birth strike. . . ."

PUSHING FOR INDEPENDENCE

The *Rebel* devoted most of its space to calls for autonomy for women. Sanger believed that a great revolution was building in women's expectations about themselves. This awakening had found expression in renewed demands for the vote. But suffrage, Sanger argued, was a superficial reform and had little appeal to the working woman. More advanced women believed in changes "more psychological" in effect. They wanted "the right to work! the right to ignore fashions, the right to keep her [*sic*] own name, and such poor longings of a bourgeois class suffering for loss of vitality." Sanger knew many cloak makers, scrubwomen, domestics, and shop workers, "who would gladly change places with those women who wanted the right to work." Successful professional women like Katharine B. Davis, New York City's commissioner of corrections, treated radical women just as harshly as male officials. Women social workers tried to teach working-class women "a slave morality" of courtesy, punctuality, loyalty, honesty, duty, "ask no questions but obey when you are told." This kind of philanthropy sought to make "these girls a tame, lifeless, spirit-less mass without personality or life—and as Nietzsche says, a guilty-grunting domestic animal." Sanger wanted to provide a counterpropaganda, to teach the working woman "only to sell her labor to the boss—not her morality—It's none of his busi-ness if she's courteous, loyal, honest, dutiful, obedient." Just as the working woman had to "fight for this right to retain her own morality and psychology—so must she fight for the right to own and control her own body . . . to do with it as she de-sires—and it's no one's business what those desires may be."

UNKNOWN ALLIES

While denouncing the "slave morality" of the middle class, Sanger expected liberated women to adhere to a demanding code of conduct. Self-rule "naturally involves a high standard of idealism as well as knowledge of the prevention of dis-ease and conception. It is none of Society's business what a woman shall do with her body unless she should inflict upon Society the consequences of her acts, like venereal disease or offspring—then Society is concerned and it is its right to be concerned." Her essential demand was that women be allowed to become free moral individuals, self-directed in both work and their relationships with others. Most of the do-gooders she despised intended no less. During the 1920s, Katharine B. Davis, as director of the Rockefeller-funded Bureau of Social Hygiene, played an important part in enlightened efforts to make information on venereal disease and contraception avail-able to working women. In 1914, however, Sanger saw only hypocrisy in both institutionalized reform and accepted stan-dards of sexual conduct. Her demand for birth control was a first step in a revolt against the paternalistic feminine models imposed by a petrified social code. She insisted that the energy released as women learned to develop their special sensibilities and powers would remake society. Just how was not clear. For the moment hatred of the existing order made its transformation seem inevitable.

WANTED BY THE LAW

Postal authorities declared the first issue of *The Woman Rebel* unmailable even though no specific contraceptive advice had been given. By mailing the journal in small batches all over the city, Sanger evaded the Post Office censorship. Subscriptions increased rapidly, letters came in from feminists all over the world, and she prepared *Family Limitation,* a pamphlet providing detailed contraceptive information. The federal government indicted Sanger for violation of the postal code after the August issue of *Rebel* carried an article on assassination that "was vague, inane, and innocuous, and had no bearing on my policy except to taunt the Government to take action." Facing a possible forty-five years in prison on nine counts of violating the federal law against mailing obscene material, she found a radical printer willing to take a "Sing Sing job" and had 10,000 copies of *Family Limitation* printed, bundled, and prepared for release. When the judge refused to postpone her trial, she left for Europe in October 1914, leaving the children with Bill [Sanger's husband], who had just returned from France. She wired her friends from aboard ship to release *Family Limitation.*

When Sanger returned to the United States in 1916, her case had been widely publicized, and the government refused to prosecute. But by then she had decided to open a birth control clinic. The guardians of public morality were to have no rest.

The Problem That Had No Name

BETTY FRIEDAN

The 1963 publication of Betty Friedan's book *The Feminine Mystique* is usually taken to mark the start of what is known as the second wave of American feminism. Indeed, the noted futurist Alvin Toffler called it "the book that pulled the trigger on history," and in the first chapter, excerpted here, Friedan outlines what she called "the problem that has no name." According to Friedan, in the late 1940s and throughout the 1950s women were bombarded with images in the mass media that told them that they belonged in the home, dedicated to husband and family. They turned to this role with fervor, Friedan argues, until it gradually became clear that a malaise had settled upon middle–class women in America. Depressed and dissatisfied, she notes, women in America had a nameless problem that doctors, psychologists, advice columnists, and others were helpless to identify. In this piece, Friedan outlines the problem and diagnoses its cause as rooted in the "feminine mystique," a set of ideals and attitudes which, as she sees it, lock women in unfulfilling roles.

T he problem lay buried, unspoken, for many years in the minds of American women. It was a strange stirring, a sense of dissatisfaction, a yearning that women suffered in the middle of the twentieth century in the United States. Each suburban wife struggled with it alone. As she made the beds, shopped for groceries, matched slipcover material, ate peanut butter sandwiches with her children, chauffeured Cub Scouts and Brownies, lay beside her husband at night—she was afraid to ask even of herself the silent question—"Is this all?"

For over fifteen years there was no word of this yearning in the millions of words written about women, for women, in all the columns, books and articles by experts telling women their role was to seek fulfillment as wives and mothers. Over and over women heard in voices of tradition and of Freudian sophistication that they could desire no greater destiny than to glory in their own femininity. Experts told them how to catch a man and keep him, how to breastfeed children and handle their toilet training, how to cope with sibling rivalry and adolescent rebellion; how to buy a dishwasher, bake bread, cook gourmet snails, and build a swimming pool with their own hands; how to dress, look, and act more feminine and make marriage more exciting; how to keep their husbands from dying young and their sons from growing into delinquents. They were taught to pity the neurotic, unfeminine, unhappy women who wanted to be poets or physicists or presidents. They learned that truly feminine women do not want careers, higher education, political rights—the independence and the opportunities that the old-fashioned feminists fought for. Some women, in their forties and fifties, still remembered painfully giving up those dreams, but most of the younger women no longer even thought about them. A thousand expert voices applauded their femininity, their adjustment, their new maturity. All they had to do was devote their lives from earliest girlhood to finding a husband and bearing children.

A FOCUS ON THE FAMILY

By the end of the nineteen-fifties, the average marriage age of women in America dropped to 20, and was still dropping, into the teens. Fourteen million girls were engaged by 17. The proportion of women attending college in comparison with men dropped from 47 per cent in 1920 to 35 per cent in 1958. A century earlier, women had fought for higher education; now girls went to college to get a husband. By the mid-fifties, 60 per cent dropped out of college to marry, or because they were afraid too much education would be a marriage bar. Colleges built dormitories for "married students," but the students were almost always the husbands. A new degree was instituted for the wives—"Ph.T." (Putting Husband Through).

Then American girls began getting married in high school. And the women's magazines, deploring the unhappy statistics about these young marriages, urged that courses on marriage, and marriage counselors, be installed in the high schools. Girls started going steady at twelve and thirteen, in junior high. Manufacturers put out brassieres with false bosoms of foam rubber for little girls of ten. And an advertisement for a child's dress, sizes 3–6x, in the *New York Times* in the fall of 1960, said: "She Too Can Join the Man-Trap Set."

THE BABY BOOM

By the end of the fifties, the United States birthrate was overtaking India's. The birth-control movement, renamed Planned Parenthood, was asked to find a method whereby women who had been advised that a third or fourth baby would be born dead or defective might have it anyhow. Statisticians were especially astounded at the fantastic increase in the number of babies among college women. Where once they had two children, now they had four, five, six. Women who had once wanted careers were now making careers out of having babies. So rejoiced *Life* magazine in a 1956 paean to the movement of American women back to the home.

In a New York hospital, a woman had a nervous breakdown when she found she could not breastfeed her baby. In other hospitals, women dying of cancer refused a drug which research had proved might save their lives: its side effects were said to be unfeminine. "If I have only one life, let me live it as a blonde," a larger-than-life-sized picture of a pretty, vacuous woman proclaimed from newspaper, magazine, and drugstore ads. And across America, three out of every ten women dyed their hair blonde. They ate a chalk called Metrecal, instead of food, to shrink to the size of the thin young models. Department-store buyers reported that American women, since 1939, had become three and four sizes smaller. "Women are out to fit the clothes, instead of vice-versa," one buyer said.

Interior decorators were designing kitchens with mosaic

murals and original paintings, for kitchens were once again the center of women's lives. Home sewing became a million-dollar industry. Many women no longer left their homes, except to shop, chauffeur their children, or attend a social engagement with their husbands. Girls were growing up in America without ever having jobs outside the home. In the late fifties, a sociological phenomenon was suddenly remarked: a third of American women now worked, but most were no longer young and very few were pursuing careers. They were married women who held part-time jobs, selling or secretarial, to put their husbands through school, their sons through college, or to help pay the mortgage. Or they were widows supporting families. Fewer and fewer women were entering professional work. The shortages in the nursing, social work, and teaching professions caused crises in almost every American city. Concerned over the Soviet Union's lead in the space race, scientists noted that America's greatest source of unused brainpower was women. But girls would not study physics: it was "unfeminine." A girl refused a science fellowship at Johns Hopkins to take a job in a real-estate office. All she wanted, she said, was what every other American girl wanted—to get married, have four children and live in a nice house in a nice suburb.

A New Ideal

The suburban housewife—she was the dream image of the young American women and the envy, it was said, of women all over the world. The American housewife—freed by science and labor-saving appliances from the drudgery, the dangers of childbirth and the illnesses of her grandmother. She was healthy, beautiful, educated, concerned only about her husband, her children, her home. She had found true feminine fulfillment. As a housewife and mother, she was respected as a full and equal partner to man in his world. She was free to choose automobiles, clothes, appliances, supermarkets; she had everything that women ever dreamed of.

In the fifteen years after World War II, this mystique of feminine fulfillment became the cherished and self-perpetuating core of contemporary American culture. Millions of women lived their lives in the image of those pretty pictures of the American suburban housewife, kissing their husbands goodbye in front of the picture window, depositing their stationwagonsful of children at school, and smiling as they ran the new electric waxer over the spotless kitchen floor. They baked their own bread, sewed their own and their children's clothes, kept their new washing machines and dryers running all day. They changed the sheets on the beds twice a week instead of once, took the rug-hooking class in adult education, and pitied their poor frustrated mothers, who had dreamed of having a career. Their only dream was to be perfect wives and mothers; their highest ambition to have five children and a beautiful house, their only fight to get and keep their husbands. They had no thought for the unfeminine problems of the world outside the home; they wanted the men to make the major decisions. They gloried in their role as women, and wrote proudly on the census blank: "Occupation: housewife."

DENYING THE PROBLEM

For over fifteen years, the words written for women, and the words women used when they talked to each other, while their husbands sat on the other side of the room and talked shop or politics or septic tanks, were about problems with their children, or how to keep their husbands happy, or improve their children's school, or cook chicken or make slipcovers. Nobody argued whether women were inferior or superior to men; they were simply different. Words like "emancipation" and "career" sounded strange and embarrassing; no one had used them for years. When a Frenchwoman named Simone de Beauvoir wrote a book called *The Second Sex,* an American critic commented that she obviously "didn't know what life was all about," and besides, she was talking about French women. The "woman problem" in America no longer existed.

If a woman had a problem in the 1950's and 1960's, she knew that something must be wrong with her marriage, or with herself. Other women were satisfied with their lives, she thought. What kind of a woman was she if she did not feel this mysterious fulfillment waxing the kitchen floor? She was so ashamed to admit her dissatisfaction that she never knew how many other women shared it. If she tried to tell her husband, he didn't understand what she was talking about. She did not really understand it herself. For over fifteen years women in America found it harder to talk about this problem than about sex. Even the psychoanalysts had no name for it. When a woman went to a psychiatrist for help, as many women did, she would say, "I'm so ashamed," or "I must be hopelessly neurotic." "I don't know what's wrong with women today," a suburban psychiatrist said uneasily. "I only know something is wrong because most of my patients happen to be women. And their problem isn't sexual." Most women with this problem did not go to see a psychoanalyst, however. "There's nothing wrong really," they kept telling themselves. "There isn't any problem." . . .

In 1960, the problem that has no name burst like a boil through the image of the happy American housewife. In the television commercials the pretty housewives still beamed over their foaming dishpans and *Time*'s cover story on "The Suburban Wife, an American Phenomenon" protested: "Having too good a time . . . to believe that they should be unhappy." But the actual unhappiness of the American housewife was suddenly being reported—from the *New York Times* and *Newsweek* to *Good Housekeeping* and CBS Television ("The Trapped Housewife"), although almost everybody who talked about it found some superficial reason to dismiss it. It was attributed to incompetent appliance repairmen (*New York Times*), or the distances children must be chauffeured in the suburbs (*Time*), or too much PTA [Parent-Teacher Association] (*Redbook*). Some said it was the old problem—education: more and more women had education, which naturally made them unhappy in their role as housewives. "The road from Freud to Frigidaire, from Sophocles to Spock, has turned out to be a bumpy one," reported the *New York Times* (June 28, 1960). "Many young women—certainly not all—whose education plunged them into a world of ideas feel stifled in their homes. They find their routine lives out of joint with their training. Like shut-ins, they feel left out. In the last year [1962], the problem of the educated housewife has provided the meat of dozens of speeches made by troubled presidents of women's colleges who maintain, in the face of complaints, that sixteen years of academic training is realistic preparation for wifehood and motherhood."

SYMPATHY WITHOUT UNDERSTANDING

There was much sympathy for the educated housewife. ("Like a two-headed schizophrenic . . . once she wrote a paper on the Graveyard poets; now she writes notes to the milkman. Once she determined the boiling point of sulphuric acid; now she determines her boiling point with the overdue repairman. . . . The housewife often is reduced to screams and tears. . . . No one, it seems, is appreciative, least of all herself, of the kind of person she becomes in the process of turning from poetess into shrew.")

Home economists suggested more realistic preparation for housewives, such as high-school workshops in home appliances. College educators suggested more discussion groups on home management and the family, to prepare women for the adjustment to domestic life. A spate of articles appeared in the mass magazines offering "Fifty-eight Ways to Make Your Marriage More Exciting." No month went by without a new book by a psychiatrist or sexologist offering technical advice on finding greater fulfillment through sex.

A male humorist joked in *Harper's Bazaar* (July, 1960) that the problem could be solved by taking away woman's right to vote. ("In the pre-19th Amendment era, the American woman was placid, sheltered and sure of her role in American society. She left all the political decisions to her husband and he, in turn, left all the family decisions to her. Today a woman has to make both the family *and* the political decisions, and it's too much for her.")

A number of educators suggested seriously that women no

longer be admitted to the four-year colleges and universities: in the growing college crisis, the education which girls could not use as housewives was more urgently needed than ever by boys to do the work of the atomic age.

DRASTIC SOLUTIONS

The problem was also dismissed with drastic solutions no one could take seriously. (A woman writer proposed in *Harper's* that women be drafted for compulsory service as nurses' aides and baby-sitters.) And it was smoothed over with the age-old panaceas: "love is their answer," "the only answer is inner help," "the secret of completeness—children," "a private means of intellectual fulfillment," "to cure this toothache of the spirit— the simple formula of handing one's self and one's will over to God."

The problem was dismissed by telling the housewife she doesn't realize how lucky she is—her own boss, no time clock, no junior executive gunning for her job. What if she isn't happy—does she think men are happy in this world? Does she really, secretly, still want to be a man? Doesn't she know yet how lucky she is to be a woman?

The problem was also, and finally, dismissed by shrugging that there are no solutions: this is what being a woman means, and what is wrong with American women that they can't accept their role gracefully? . . .

But those who had faced it honestly knew that all the superficial remedies, the sympathetic advice, the scolding words and the cheering words were somehow drowning the problem in unreality. A bitter laugh was beginning to be heard from American women. They were admired, envied, pitied, theorized over until they were sick of it, offered drastic solutions or silly choices that no one could take seriously. They got all kinds of advice from the growing armies of marriage and child-guidance counselors, psychotherapists, and armchair psychologists, on how to adjust to their role as housewives. No other road to fulfillment was offered to American women in the middle of the twentieth century. Most adjusted to their role and suffered or ignored the problem that has no name. It can be less painful, for a woman, not to hear the strange, dissatisfied voice stirring within her.

A Voice of Dissatisfaction

It is no longer possible to ignore that voice, to dismiss the desperation of so many American women. This is not what being a woman means, no matter what the experts say. For human suffering there is a reason; perhaps the reason has not been found because the right questions have not been asked, or pressed far enough. I do not accept the answer that there is no problem because American women have luxuries that women in other times and lands never dreamed of; part of the strange newness of the problem is that it cannot be understood in terms of the age-old material problems of man: poverty, sickness, hunger, cold. The women who suffer this problem have a hunger that food cannot fill. It persists in women whose husbands are struggling internes and law clerks, or prosperous doctors and lawyers; in wives of workers and executives who make $5,000 a year or $50,000. It is not caused by lack of material advantages; it may not even be felt by women preoccupied with desperate problems of hunger, poverty or illness. And women who think it will be solved by more money, a bigger house, a second car, moving to a better suburb, often discover it gets worse.

It is no longer possible today to blame the problem on loss of femininity: to say that education and independence and equality with men have made American women unfeminine. I have heard so many women try to deny this dissatisfied voice within themselves because it does not fit the pretty picture of femininity the experts have given them. I think, in fact, that this is the first clue to the mystery: the problem cannot be understood in the generally accepted terms by which scientists have studied women, doctors have treated them, counselors have advised them, and writers have written about them. Women who suffer this problem, in whom this voice is stirring, have lived their whole lives in the pursuit of feminine fulfillment. They are not career women (although career women may have other problems); they are women whose greatest ambition has been marriage and children. For the oldest of these women, these daughters of the American middle class, no other dream was possible. The ones in their forties and fifties who once had other dreams gave them up and threw themselves joyously into life as housewives. For the youngest, the new wives and mothers, this was the only dream. They are the ones who quit high school and college to marry, or marked time in some job in which they had no real interest until they married. These women are very "feminine" in the usual sense, and yet they still suffer the problem. . . .

INVISIBLE PRISONS

It is easy to see the concrete details that trap the suburban housewife, the continual demands on her time. But the chains that bind her in her trap are chains in her own mind and spirit. They are chains made up of mistaken ideas and misinterpreted facts, of incomplete truths and unreal choices. They are not easily seen and not easily shaken off.

How can any woman see the whole truth within the bounds of her own life? How can she believe that voice inside herself, when it denies the conventional, accepted truths by which she has been living? And yet the women I have talked to, who are finally listening to that inner voice, seem in some incredible way to be groping through to a truth that has defied the experts.

I think the experts in a great many fields have been holding pieces of that truth under their microscopes for a long time without realizing it. I found pieces of it in certain new research and theoretical developments in psychological, social and biological science whose implications for women seem never to have been examined. I found many clues by talking to suburban doctors, gynecologists, obstetricians, child-guidance clinicians, pediatricians, high-school guidance counselors, college professors, marriage counselors, psychiatrists and ministers—questioning them not on their theories, but on their actual experience in treating American women. I became aware of a growing body of evidence, much of which has not been reported publicly because it does not fit current modes of thought about women—evidence which throws into question the standards of feminine normality, feminine adjustment, feminine fulfillment, and feminine maturity by which most women are still trying to live.

WHERE THE PROBLEM LIES

I began to see in a strange new light the American return to early marriage and the large families that are causing the population explosion; the recent movement to natural childbirth and breastfeeding; suburban conformity, and the new neuroses, character pathologies and sexual problems being reported by the doctors. I began to see new dimensions to old problems that have long been taken for granted among women: menstrual difficulties, sexual frigidity, promiscuity, pregnancy fears, childbirth depression, the high incidence of emotional breakdown and suicide among women in their twenties and thirties, the menopause crises, the so-called passivity and immaturity of American men, the discrepancy between women's tested intellectual abilities in childhood and their adult achievement, the changing incidence of adult sexual orgasm in American women, and persistent problems in psychotherapy and in women's education.

If I am right, the problem that has no name stirring in the minds of so many American women today is not a matter of loss of femininity or too much education, or the demands of domesticity. It is far more important than anyone recognizes. It is the key to these other new and old problems which have been torturing women and their husbands and children, and puzzling their doctors and educators for years. It may well be the key to our future as a nation and a culture. We can no longer ignore that voice within women that says: "I want something more than my husband and my children and my home."

Women's Liberation Aims to Free Men Too

GLORIA STEINEM

In this piece, Gloria Steinem, a prominent feminist, argues that the women's movement is good for everyone, including men. She argues that old, established patterns of behavior have to be unlearned, and that myths about the proper roles and capacities of men and women must be abandoned. Although this is not an easy task, she says, it is a necessary one, for it is only when people see the true character of the world in which they live that they can see where it needs improving.

According to Steinem, American society suffers not merely from sexism but also from elitism, racism, and violence. She argues that feminism, by emphasizing the need to reject old myths in order to create a better society, can help unite Americans in a struggle against injustice, in whatever form it may appear. In this way, she says, feminism will benefit everyone, regardless of his or her gender. The feminist movement is best viewed as a major humanist movement, according to Steinem, ushering in a new era of peace, understanding, and social justice, rather than as an isolated, fringe activity designed to benefit a privileged few.

This is the year of Women's Liberation. Or at least, it's the year the press has discovered a movement that has been strong for several years now, and reported it as a small, privileged, rather lunatic event instead of the major revolution in consciousness—in everyone's consciousness, male or female—that I believe it truly is.

It is a movement that some call "feminist" but should more

accurately be called humanist; a movement that is an integral part of rescuing this country from its old, expensive patterns of elitism, racism and violence.

The first problem for all of us, men and women, is not to learn, but to unlearn. We are filled with the popular wisdom of several centuries just past, and we are terrified to give it up. Patriotism means obedience, age means wisdom, woman means submission, black means inferior: these are preconceptions imbedded so deeply in our thinking that we honestly may not know that they are there.

Unfortunately, authorities who write textbooks are sometimes subject to the same popular wisdom as the rest of us. They gather their proof around it, and end by becoming the theoreticians of the status quo. Using the most respectable of scholarly methods, for instance, English scientists proved definitively that the English were descended from the angels while the Irish were descended from the apes.

GETTING RID OF OLD MYTHS

It was beautifully done, complete with comparative skull measurements, and it was a rationale for the English domination of the Irish for more than 100 years. I try to remember that when I'm reading Arthur Jensen's current and very impressive work on the limitations of black intelligence, or when I'm reading Lionel Tiger on the inability of women to act in groups.

It wasn't easy for the English to give up their mythic superiority. Indeed, there are quite a few Irish who doubt that they have done it yet. Clearing our minds and government policies of outdated myths is proving to be at least as difficult, but it is also inevitable. Whether it's woman's secondary role in society or the paternalistic role of the United States in the world, the old assumptions just don't work any more.

Part of living this revolution is having the scales fall from our eyes. Every day we see small obvious truths that we had missed before. Our histories, for instance, have generally been written for and about white men. Inhabited countries were "discovered" when the first white male set foot there, and most of us learned more about any one European country than we did about Africa and Asia combined.

I confess that, before some consciousness-changing of my own, I would have thought that the women's history courses springing up around the country belonged in the same cultural ghetto as home economics. The truth is that we need Women's studies almost as much as we need Black studies, and for exactly the same reason: too many of us have completed a "good" education believing that everything from political power to scientific discovery was the province of white males.

We believed, for instance, that the vote had been "given" to women in some whimsical, benevolent fashion. We never learned about the long desperation of the women's struggle, or about the strength and wisdom of the women who led it. We knew a great deal more about the outdated, male supremacist theories of Sigmund Freud than we did about societies where women had equal responsibility, or even ruled.

"Anonymous," Virginia Woolf once said sadly, "was a woman."

A COMPARISON WITH RACISM

I don't mean to equate our problems of identity with those that flowed from slavery. But, as Gunnar Myrdal pointed out in his classic study "An American Dilemma," "In drawing a parallel between the position of, and feeling toward, women and Negroes, we are uncovering a fundamental basis of our culture."

Blacks and women suffer from the same myths of childlike natures; smaller brains; inability to govern themselves, much less white men; limited job skills; identity as sex objects, and so on. Ever since slaves arrived on these shores and were given the legal status of wives—that is, chattel—our legal reforms have followed on each other's heels—with women, I might add, still lagging considerably behind.

President Nixon's Commission on women concluded that the Supreme Court sanctions discrimination against women—discrimination that it long ago ruled unconstitutional in the case of blacks—but the commission report remains mysteriously unreleased by the White House. An equal rights amendment now up again before the Senate has been delayed by a male-chauvinist Congress for 47 years. Neither blacks nor women have role-models in history: models of individuals who have been honored in authority outside the home.

As Margaret Mead [a well-known American anthropologist] has noted, the only women allowed to be dominant and respectable at the same time are widows. You have to do what society wants you to do, have a husband who dies, and then have power thrust upon you through no fault of your own. The whole thing seems very hard on the men.

Before we go on to other reasons why Women's Liberation Is Men's Liberation, too—and why this incarnation of the women's movement is inseparable from the larger revolution— perhaps we should clear the air of a few more myths—the myth that women are biologically inferior, for instance. In fact, an equally good case could be made for the reverse.

WOMEN ARE NOT BIOLOGICALLY INFERIOR

Women live longer than man. That's when the groups being studied are always being cited as proof that we work them to death, but the truth is that women live longer than men even when the groups being studied are monks and nuns. We survived Nazi concentration camps better, are protected against heart attacks by our female hormones, are less subject to many diseases, withstand surgery better and are so much more durable at every stage of life that nature conceives 20 to 50 per cent more males just to keep the balance going.

The Auto Safety Committee of the American Medical Association has come to the conclusion that women are better drivers because they're less emo-

Gloria Steinem in 1970

tional than men. I never thought I would hear myself quoting the AMA, but that one was too good to resist.

I don't want to prove the superiority of one sex to another: that would only be repeating a male mistake. The truth is that we're just not sure how many of our differences are biological and how many are societal. What we do know is that the differences between the two sexes, like the differences between races, are much less great than the differences to be found within each group.

WOMEN ARE NOT TREATED EQUALLY

A second myth is that women are already being treated equally in this society. We ourselves have been guilty of perpetuating this myth, especially at upper economic levels where women have grown fond of being lavishly maintained as ornaments and children. The chains may be made of mink and wall-to-wall carpeting, but they are still chains.

The truth is that a woman with a college degree working full time makes less than a black man with a high school degree working full time. And black women make least of all. In many parts of the country—New York City, for instance—a woman has no legally guaranteed right to rent an apartment, buy a house, get accommodations in a hotel or be served in a public restaurant. She can be refused simply because of her sex.

In some states, women get longer jail sentences for the same crime. Women on welfare must routinely answer humiliating personal questions; male welfare recipients do not. A woman is the last to be hired, the first to be fired. Equal pay for equal work is the exception. Equal chance for advancement, especially at upper levels or at any level with authority over men, is rare enough to be displayed in a museum.

As for our much-touted economic power, *we* make up only 5 per cent of the Americans receiving $10,000 a year or more, and that includes all the famous rich widows. We are 51 per cent of all stockholders, a dubious honor these days, but we hold only 18 per cent of the stock—and that is generally controlled by men.

In fact, the myth of economic matriarchy in this country is less testimony to our power than to resentment of the little power we do have.

You may wonder why we have submitted to such humiliations all these years; why, indeed, women will sometimes deny that they are second-class citizens at all. The answer lies in the psychology of second-classness. Like all such groups, we come to accept what society says about us. We believe that we can make it in the world only by "Uncle Tom-ing," by a real or pretended subservience to white males.

Even when we come to understand that we, as individuals, are not second class, we still accept society's assessment of our group—a phenomenon psychologists refer to as internalized aggression. From this stems the desire to be the only woman in an office, an academic department or any other part of the man's world. From this also stems women who put down their sisters—and my own profession of journalism has some of them.

I don't want to give the impression, though, that we want to join society exactly as it is. I don't think most women want to pick up briefcases and march off to meaningless, depersonalized jobs. Nor do we want to be drafted—and women certainly should be drafted; even the readers of *Seventeen* magazine were recently polled as being overwhelmingly in favor of women in national service—to serve in a war like the one in Indochina.

A BETTER LIFE FOR EVERYONE

We want to liberate men from those inhuman roles as well. We want to share the work and responsibility, and to have men share equal responsibility for the children. Probably the ultimate myth is that children must have fulltime mothers, and that liberated women make bad ones. The truth is that most American children seem to be suffering from too much mother and too little father.

Women now spend more time with their homes and families than in any other past or present society we know about. To get back to the sanity of the agrarian or joint family system, we need free universal day care. With that aid, as in Scandinavian countries, and with laws that permit women equal work and equal pay, man will be relieved of his role as sole breadwinner and stranger to his own children.

No more alimony. Fewer boring wives. Fewer childlike wives. No more so-called "Jewish mothers," who are simply normally ambitious human beings with all their ambitiousness confined to the house. No more wives who fall apart with the first wrinkle because they've been taught that their total identity depends on their outsides. No more responsibility for another adult human being who has never been told she is responsible for her own life, and who sooner or later says some version of, "If I hadn't married you, I could have been a star." Women's Liberation really is Men's Liberation, too.

The family system that will emerge is a great subject of anxiety. Probably there will be a variety of choices. Colleague marriages, such as young people have now, with both partners going to law-school or the Peace Corps together, is one alternative. At least they share more than the kitchen and the bedroom. Communes; marriages that are valid for the child-rearing years only—there are many possibilities.

The point is that Women's Liberation is not destroying the American family. It is trying to build a human compassionate alternative out of its ruins.

BRINGING PEOPLE TOGETHER

One final myth that women are more moral than men. We are not more moral; we are only uncorrupted by power. But until the old generation of male chauvinists is out of office women in positions of power can increase our chances of peace a great deal.

I personally would rather have had Margaret Mead as President during the past six years of Vietnam than either Lyndon Johnson or Richard Nixon. At least she wouldn't have had her masculinity to prove. Much of the trouble this country is in has to do with the masculine mystique: The idea that manhood somehow depends on the subjugation of other people. It's a bipartisan problem.

The challenge to all of us is to live a revolution, not to die for one. There has been too much killing, and the weapons are now far too terrible. This revolution has to change consciousness, to upset the injustice of our current hierarchy by refusing to honor it. And it must be a life that enforces a new social justice.

Because the truth is that none of us can be liberated if other groups are not. Women's Liberation is a bridge between black and white women, but also between the construction workers and the suburbanites, between Mr. Nixon's Silent Majority [that part of society that wasn't active in the protests of the late 1960s] and the young people it fears. Indeed, there's much more injustice and rage among working-class women than among the much publicized white radicals.

Women are sisters; they have many of the same problems, and they can communicate with each other. "You only get radicalized," as black activists always told us, "on your own thing." Then we make the connection to other injustices in society. The women's movement is an important revolutionary bridge, and we are building it.

Lesbianism and the Women's Liberation Movement

MARTHA SHELLEY

Martha Shelley was a prominent activist in the feminist and gay rights movements of the 1960s and 1970s. In this article, she argues that important connections exist between lesbianism and feminism. According to Shelley, both lesbianism and feminism are about valuing women, and, just as important, each calls for the rejection of female dependence on men. As Shelley sees it, women are oppressed by men and men have no real love or respect for women. Consequently, Shelley believes, if the women's rights movement is to succeed, women have to look to each other for love and support. Although Shelley grants that the ultimate goal is a loving society in which a person's gender doesn't matter, she argues that this future goal must not lead women to overlook the fact that, currently, men are violent and hateful toward women.

The worst epithets used against women in the Women's Liberation Movement have been (and still are) "lesbian" and "manhater." I shall attempt here to examine what these names mean—why most women fear these labels, and why they have been so effectively used against women.

Men don't like uppity women. They don't like independent women—women who make as much money as they do, women who are as well-educated, as mobile, as free in their actions. They don't like women who aren't dependent on them—who aren't sitting at home waiting for the phone to ring, waiting for "him" to come home, women who don't feel

Excerpted from "Lesbianism and the Women's Liberation Movement," by Martha Shelley, *Women's Liberation: Blueprint for the Future* (New York: Ace Books, 1970).

totally crushed at the thought that some man doesn't love them anymore, women who are not terrified at the idea that a man might leave them.

So we must have two definitions for the lesbian—one in terms of her sexual relations, the other in terms of her independence of men. There are many lesbians who enjoy the company of men and who are lesbian in sexual practice only. There are many women who are celibate, but who would be perfectly happy if all men were exiled to Outer Mongolia and reproduction were carried on by means of artificial insemination.

The physical and economic oppression of women could not be carried on so effectively without a corresponding psychological oppression, the indoctrination of women which results in their desperate need for men's approval. Men are not so dependent on women—it is considered shameful for a man to refrain from a course of action simply because his wife wouldn't approve. He may keep some actions secret (such as sexual affairs) in order to keep peace in the household—but his psychological well-being does not depend on his wife's frame of mind. He is not really upset if she forgets his birthday—although he may be annoyed if he feels that she is not giving him the respect due to her lord and master. Her lack of consideration may provoke him into finding another slave.

His lack of consideration is something she blames herself for, something she feels she must bear, in spite of her feeling of utter desolation.

THE THREAT OF INDEPENDENT WOMEN

A woman who doesn't care what men think of her—ah, this is dangerous. This is the worst conceivable insult to the male ego. Some men find true lesbianism impossible to imagine. I once knew a fellow who believed that when two women made love, they imagined that a man was watching them. He simply could not conceive that women could function at all without a male presence. I suspect that most men who enjoy watching pornographic films about "lesbians" have his turn of mind. Most heterosexual men cannot endure watching films about male homosexuals—they find it "disgusting," "unexciting," "repulsive;" in other words, too threatening.

This attitude on the part of men has actually protected the lesbian to some degree. The male homosexual has endured much more in the way of physical persecution than the female—because straight men must at all costs eradicate the homosexual in themselves. But they don't take women seriously enough to consider lesbianism a real threat—or didn't until the Women's Liberation Movement came along. As women become more independent, I suspect that violence against us will increase.

FACING CHALLENGES

Most lesbians have always attempted to live secretly. The few who are obvious in appearance are despised by gay and straight communities alike. Yet this schizophrenic existence takes its toll psychologically. It may be true that a higher percentage of homosexuals end up in mental institutions—driven there not by homosexuality, but by the knowledge that one slip could cost them their jobs, their education, their family and friends. Those few who are recognizable are despised under the rationale, "You shouldn't advertise what you do in bed." Those people who collapsed under the strain were simply unable to take the deception that most of us have had to live with. It isn't what you do in bed that matters so much—but the fact that you can't walk down the street holding the hand of someone you love, you can't announce to your family, your friends, your world, "This is my beloved."

The lesbian has needed more strength than most in order to survive. Besides having to develop a sense of self-esteem that can withstand intense disapproval, besides having to retain her sanity, she also has had to survive economically without the aid of men. As a result, there have been a disproportionate number of lesbians among successful women. Many of us have fought against tremendous odds to get a decent education and decent jobs. Women who need male approval have an even harder time making it in the face of men's anger at their successes.

We pay heavily for our successes, as well as for our failures. A successful woman is considered a lesbian, whatever her sexual preferences. The only way she can combat this stigma is by putting other women down and playing up to men, thus reassuring them that whatever her income, whatever her position, she still needs male approval. As for failures, if a lesbian drinks heavily or takes pills, this is ascribed to her homosexuality. No one but the most unreconstructed racist would say that black people who take drugs or commit violent acts are violent because they are black; yet men consider the self-destructiveness of homosexuals to be a result of their homosexuality, not a result of their oppression.

And men love nothing better than to hear the story of a lesbian who committed suicide.

PUSHED INTO THERAPY

We all know how psychoanalysis is used against women to pressure them into conforming to their roles. This is particularly true in the case of the lesbian. The psychoanalyst, in this case, considers it his duty to "cure" her, i.e., to make her go straight. All her woes are ascribed to her homosexuality. Translated into street language, his sophisticated terminology boils down to "All she needs is a good fuck." Any changes which take place in the course of therapy, which result in her living a happier life as a lesbian, are considered as making an adjustment to a regrettable but untreatable condition. If the psychoanalyst gets the patient to state that she enjoys intercourse with men, hallelujah, he's a success!—she has been turned into a woman who needs male approval. If he fails, she was probably too far gone, and anyway, he did the best he could.

Another interesting psychoanalytic myth is that of "stages of development." It is held by some neo-Freudians that everyone passes through a homosexual period in early adolescence, and that some people become "arrested" at the homosexual stage. The heterosexual has apparently passed through that stage of development and has "put away childish things." Now let us take this theory as it is explained by its more sophisticated exponents. A homosexual period is not defined merely in terms of genital behavior, but in terms of those whom one loves. Therefore, a young person who deeply loves her best friend is considered to be passing through such a period. Someone who has genital relationships with the opposite sex but can only form enduring friendships with the same sex could not be considered a "mature" heterosexual.

HETEROSEXUAL RELATIONSHIPS

I used to subscribe to this theory until it became apparent to me that there is very little love between men and women, and that most heterosexual relationships are based on a master-slave psychology which can hardly be said to characterize mature adulthood. Most relationships called "mature" by psychoanalysts are also relationships which would be acceptable to the most orthodox church-monogamous marriages, with the male as the head of the household. So this psychoanalytic construct ends up meaning that you can fool around in your youth, but you must end up "saved."

Since most heterosexuals are so frightened of homosexuality, it is hard to believe that they have successfully passed through a homosexual stage—indeed, it seems more likely that they have totally avoided the possibility of love for their own sex. And if it is true that you cannot love others until you love yourself, and that you cannot love people who are different from you (different sex, different race, different culture) until you love those who are like yourself, then it seems to me that there is very little love in the world indeed. A glance at this morning's paper confirms my impression.

I suppose I must go into the myth of the naturalness of heterosexual intercourse, although that argument has begun to bore me. Taken to its extreme, it means that sex is meant for reproduction, and that therefore any sexual act which cannot lead to reproduction (anal or oral intercourse, masturbation, intercourse with contraception) is perverted. The leading exponents of this extreme position are the hierarchy of the Roman Catholic Church. The more sophisticated position of the

"What Is a Lesbian?"

Radicalesbians, originally published as "The Woman-Identified Woman" in a small pamphlet/newsletter by Know, Inc.

What is a lesbian? A lesbian is the rage of all women condensed to the point of explosion. She is the woman who, often beginning at an extremely early age, acts in accordance with her inner compulsion to be a more complete and freer human being than her society—perhaps then, but certainly later—cares to allow her. These needs and actions, over a period of years, bring her into painful conflict with people, situations, the accepted ways of thinking, feeling and behaving, until she is in a state of continual war with everything around her, and usually with her self. She may not be fully conscious of the political implications of what for her began as personal necessity, but on some level she has not been able to accept the limitations and oppression laid on her by the most basic role of her society—the female role. The turmoil she experiences tends to induce guilt proportional to the degree to which she feels she is not meeting social expectations, and/or eventu-

psychoanalyst is that all methods are permissible, but that a normal person must clearly prefer "straight" sex. This totally ignores any objective surveys in the area, which show, for example, that most people masturbate more often than they perform any other sexual acts in their lives. Or that straight sex may be most satisfactory to men, but that most women have difficulty having orgasms by this method, and that there is no such "animal" as a vaginal orgasm.

A more disturbing finding by Masters and Johnson is that frigidity is extremely rare among lesbians. This could be interpreted to mean that women simply know more about women's ally drives her to question and analyze what the rest of her society more or less accepts. She is forced to evolve her own life pattern, often living much of her life alone, learning usually much earlier than her "straight" (heterosexual) sisters about the essential aloneness of life (which the myth of marriage obscures) and about the reality of illusions. To the extent that she cannot expel the heavy socialization that goes with being female, she can never truly find peace with herself. For she is caught somewhere between accepting society's view of her—in which case she cannot accept herself—and coming to understand what this sexist society has done to her and why it is functional and necessary for it to do so. Those of us who work that through find ourselves on the other side of a tortuous journey through a night that may have been decades long. The perspective gained from that journey, the liberation of self, the inner peace, the real love of self and of all women, is something to be shared with all women—because we are all women.

Radicalesbians, "The Woman-Identified Woman," in Anne Koedt (ed.), *Notes from the Third Year*. New York, 1971.

bodies than men do; or that women who don't care much for sex generally marry men for social convenience, since a relationship with a woman would give them the status of outcasts without any compensatory benefits.

LESBIANISM AND MANHATING

To me, lesbianism is not an oddity of a few women to be hidden in the background of the Movement. In a way, it is the heart of the Women's Liberation Movement. In order to throw off the oppression of the male caste, women must unite—we must learn to love ourselves and each other, we must grow strong and independent of men so that we can deal with them from a position of strength. The idea that women must teach men how to love, that we must not become man-haters is, at this point in history, like preaching pacifism to the Vietcong. Women are constantly being assaulted, raped and killed if they dare to violate the unwritten curfew that says they do not belong on the streets after certain hours, but in the homes. They are told to be weak, dependent and loving. That kind of love is masochism. Love can only exist between equals, not between the oppressed and the oppressor.

Men do not love women. They perhaps become entranced at the image of the seductress, or challenged by the woman who plays "hard to get." They do not want women as people, they want only those who fit properly into the roles of sexual and domestic slaves. Any time a woman aspires to independent personhood, the reaction of men is rage.

You don't believe it. Your man lets you go on to graduate school, is encouraging you to develop a career of your own. He wants you to work. But supposing you told him that your company wanted you to move to another city—how would he like to relocate? Wives are always supposed to relocate, not husbands.

Pick up the daily newspaper in any large city and every day you will read the story of another woman brutally raped and murdered by men. When this is done to black men by white men, it is called lynching. People no longer apologize for lynching by calling it the work of a few sick men—they recognize that lynching is the product of racism, that it is fostered by attitudes of white supremacy. The daily lynchings of women are equally the product of supremacy. They are not merely the work of a few sick individuals, but the natural outcome of a disease which affects the whole human race.

Men hate women. Some are more open about it; others are merely quietly thankful that they were not born women. And yet our whole function in life is, we are told, to love men.

The strength of an oppressed class is the love between its members, its solidarity, and its hatred of the oppressor. We are the oldest oppressed class in history—why are we afraid to hate?

Let us learn, then, to hate men, instead of hiding our rage behind a screen of placidity and niceness and pacifism. Let us not use pacifism as a screen for cowardice—even Ghandi said that it is better to have the courage of a soldier than no courage at all.

We are told that it is our job to teach men how to love, since we are so much better at it. It is not our job—not at this time—to teach men how to love. Men are not babies. Shall we continue to behave as did Uncle Tom, dying under the lash, whispering, "I love you, master—God save you"? You cannot teach while you are on your knees.

Every time a woman betrays another woman, acts bitchy for the sake of a man, she weakens the Women's Liberation Movement. Every woman whose primary loyalty is to a man draws strength away from the Movement. The lesbian is not someone for the Movement to be ashamed of, not someone to be denied, apologized for, hidden, explained away. We must stop assuring men that lesbians are in the minority, that we are mostly nice girls who really love men.

I find it very odd that I am expected to love, or at least like, men who rape my sisters. Shall I work to bring the boys home from Vietnam, our poor dear boys, so that they can turn their violence against us instead of the poor women of Mylai? I want to bring the boys home simply to end the slaughter of the Vietnamese people—but I shudder at the thought of having to deal with those whoremongers and ear-collectors when they return.

A DISTANT FUTURE

Our ultimate aim must be a loving society—one in which people can love each other regardless of sex. But we cannot confuse the future with the present. We cannot preach love to murderers and victims. We cannot pretend that it is possible to love those who torture us with their contempt, their arrogance and their violence, saying that the poor overgrown boys only act out of ignorance.

The most common reaction of "straight" women in the Movement towards their lesbian sisters has been irrational fear—the fear that we will physically attack them. Frankly, I've never heard of a homosexual attacking a heterosexual (prison rapes are usually conducted by brutalized straight men against weak or effeminate inmates). The other reaction has been that we will give the Movement a bad name—to me, this is grasping at the last straw of male approval. But more and more women in the Movement are discovering and dealing with homosexual feelings in themselves, and many are entering lesbian relationships.

I can only hope that, as the Movement grows, more and more women will come to depend on other women for emotional support, for love and comradeship. For it is only when women have ceased to fear lesbianism, have ceased to fear the consequences of their hatred for men, that we will have our liberation.

Blame It on Feminism

SUSAN FALUDI

A Pulitzer Prize–winning reporter for the *Wall Street Journal*, Susan Faludi's 1991 book *Backlash* earned her the 1991 National Book Critics Award for general nonfiction. In this work, the introduction to which is excerpted here, Faludi argues that through the 1980s a strong antifeminist chorus developed in the American media and in the public mind. According to Faludi, feminism was being blamed for various woes women in America were alleged to feel. Against this, Faludi argues that the problems women face are caused by a continuing lack of equality rather than by feminism itself. As she sees it, the criticisms she observes mark a backlash against feminism that is driven by a fear that arose when feminists began to achieve some of their goals.

To be a woman in America at the close of the 20th century—what good fortune. That's what we keep hearing, anyway. The barricades have fallen, politicians assure us. Women have "made it," Madison Avenue cheers. Women's fight for equality has "largely been won," *Time* magazine announces. Enroll at any university, join any law firm, apply for credit at any bank. Women have so many opportunities now, corporate leaders say, that we don't really need equal opportunity policies. Women are so equal now, lawmakers say, that we no longer need an Equal Rights Amendment. Women have "so much," former President Ronald Reagan says, that the White House no longer needs to appoint them to higher office. Even American Express ads are saluting a woman's freedom to charge it. At last, women have received their full citizenship papers.

And yet . . .

Behind this celebration of the American woman's victory, behind the news, cheerfully and endlessly repeated, that the struggle for women's rights is won, another message flashes. You may be free and equal now, it says to women, but you have never been more miserable.

This bulletin of despair is posted everywhere—at the newsstand, on the TV set, at the movies, in advertisements and doctors' offices and academic journals. Professional women are suffering "burnout" and succumbing to an "infertility epidemic." Single women are grieving from a "man shortage." The *New York Times* reports: Childless women are "depressed and confused" and their ranks are swelling. *Newsweek* says: Unwed women are "hysterical" and crumbling under a "profound crisis of confidence." The health advice manuals inform: Highpowered career women are stricken with unprecedented outbreaks of "stress-induced disorders," hair loss, bad nerves, alcoholism, and even heart attacks. The psychology books advise: Independent women's loneliness represents "a major mental health problem today." Even founding feminist Betty Friedan has been spreading the word: she warns that women now suffer from a new identity crisis and "new 'problems that have no name.'"

TOO MUCH FEMINISM?

How can American women be in so much trouble at the same time that they are supposed to be so blessed? If the status of women has never been higher, why is their emotional state so low? If women got what they asked for, what could possibly be the matter now?

The prevailing wisdom of the past decade [the 1980s] has supported one, and only one, answer to this riddle: it must be all that equality that's causing all that pain. Women are unhappy precisely *because* they are free. Women are enslaved by their own liberation. They have grabbed at the gold ring of independence, only to miss the one ring that really matters. They have gained control of their fertility, only to destroy it. They have pursued their own professional dreams—and lost out on the greatest female adventure. The women's movement, as we are told time and again, has proved women's own worst enemy.

"In dispensing its spoils, women's liberation has given my generation high incomes, our own cigarette, the option of single parenthood, rape crisis centers, personal lines of credit, free love, and female gynecologists," Mona Charen, a young law student, writes in the *National Review*, in an article titled "The Feminist Mistake." "In return it has effectively robbed us of one thing upon which the happiness of most women rests—men." The *National Review* is a conservative publication, but such charges against the women's movement are not confined to its pages. "Our generation was the human sacrifice" to the women's movement, *Los Angeles Times* feature writer Elizabeth Mehren contends in a *Time* cover story. Baby-boom women like her, she says, have been duped by feminism: "We believed the rhetoric." In *Newsweek,* writer Kay Ebeling dubs feminism "the Great Experiment That Failed" and asserts "women in my generation, its perpetrators, are the casualties." Even the beauty magazines are saying it: *Harper's Bazaar* accuses the women's movement of having "lost us [women] ground instead of gaining it."

PLACING THE BLAME

In the last decade, publications from the *New York Times* to *Vanity Fair* to the *Nation* have issued a steady stream of indictments against the women's movement, with such headlines as WHEN FEMINISM FAILED or THE AWFUL TRUTH ABOUT WOMEN'S LIB. They hold the campaign for women's equality responsible for nearly every woe besetting women, from mental depression to meager savings accounts, from teenage suicides to eating disorders to bad complexions. The "Today" show says women's liberation is to blame for bag ladies. A guest columnist in the *Baltimore Sun* even proposes that feminists produced the rise in slasher movies. By making the "violence" of abortion more acceptable, the author reasons, women's rights activists made it all right to show graphic murders on screen. . . .

But what "equality" are all these authorities talking about?

If American women are so equal, why do they represent two-thirds of all poor adults? Why are nearly 75 percent of full-time working women making less than $20,000 a year, nearly double the male rate? Why are they still far more likely than men to live in poor housing and receive no health insurance, and twice as likely to draw no pension? Why does the average working woman's salary still lag as far behind the average man's as it did twenty years ago? Why does the average female college graduate today earn less than a man with no more than a high school diploma (just as she did in the '50s)— and why does the average female high school graduate today earn less than a male high school dropout? Why do American women, in fact, face one of the worst gender-based pay gaps in the developed world?

An Elusive Equality

If women have "made it," then why are nearly 80 percent of working women still stuck in traditional "female" jobs—as secretaries, administrative "support" workers and salesclerks? And, conversely, why are they less than 8 percent of all federal and state judges, less than 6 percent of all law partners, and less than one half of 1 percent of top corporate managers? Why are there only three female state governors, two female U.S. senators, and two Fortune 500 chief executives? Why are only nineteen of the four thousand corporate officers and directors women—and why do more than half the boards of Fortune companies still lack even one female member?

If women "have it all," then why don't they have the most basic requirements to achieve equality in the work force? Unlike virtually all other industrialized nations, the U.S. government still has no family-leave and child care programs—and more than 99 percent of American private employers don't offer child care either. Though business leaders say they are aware of and deplore sex discrimination, corporate America has yet to make an honest effort toward eradicating it. In a 1990 national poll of chief executives at Fortune 1000 companies, more than 80 percent acknowledged that discrimination impedes female employees' progress—yet, less than 1 percent of these same companies regarded *remedying* sex discrimination as a goal that their personnel departments should pursue. In fact, when the companies' human resource officers were asked to rate their department's priorities, women's advancement ranked last.

An Incomplete Victory

If women are so "free," why are their reproductive freedoms in greater jeopardy today than a decade earlier? Why do women who want to postpone childbearing now have fewer options than ten years ago? The availability of different forms of contraception has declined, research for new birth control has virtually halted, new laws restricting abortion—or even *information* about abortion—for young and poor women have been passed, and the U.S. Supreme Court has shown little ardor in defending the right it granted in 1973.

Nor is women's struggle for equal education over; as a 1989 study found, three-fourths of all high schools still violate the federal law banning sex discrimination in education. In colleges, undergraduate women receive only 70 percent of the aid undergraduate men get in grants and work-study jobs—and women's sports programs receive a pittance compared with men's. A review of state equal-education laws in the late '80s found that only thirteen states had adopted the minimum provisions required by the federal Title IX law—and only seven states had anti-discrimination regulations that covered all education levels.

Nor do women enjoy equality in their own homes, where they still shoulder 70 percent of the household duties—and the only major change in the last fifteen years is that now middle-class men *think* they do more around the house. (In fact, a national poll finds the ranks of women saying their husbands share equally in child care shrunk to 31 percent in 1987 from 40 percent three years earlier.) Furthermore, in thirty states, it is still generally legal for husbands to rape their wives; and only ten states have laws mandating arrest for domestic violence—even though battering was the leading cause of injury of women in the late '80s. Women who have no other option but to flee find that isn't much of an alternative either. Federal funding for battered women's shelters has been withheld and one-third of the 1 million battered women who seek emergency shelter each year can find none. Blows from men contributed far more to the rising numbers of "bag ladies" than the ill effects of feminism. In the '80s, almost half of all homeless women (the fastest growing segment of the homeless) were refugees of domestic violence.

What Women Think

The word may be that women have been "liberated," but women themselves seem to feel otherwise. Repeatedly in national surveys, majorities of women say they are still far from equality. Nearly 70 percent of women polled by the *New York Times* in 1989 said the movement for women's rights had only just begun. Most women in the 1990 Virginia Slims opinion poll agreed with the statement that conditions for their sex in American society had improved "a little, not a lot." In poll after poll in the decade, overwhelming majorities of women said they needed equal pay and equal job opportunities, they needed an Equal Rights Amendment, they needed the right to an abortion without government interference, they needed a federal law guaranteeing maternity leave, they needed decent child care services. They have none of these. So how exactly have we "won" the war for women's rights?

Seen against this background, the much ballyhooed claim that feminism is responsible for making women miserable becomes absurd—and irrelevant. As we shall see in the chapters to follow, the afflictions ascribed to feminism are all myths. From "the man shortage" to "the infertility epidemic" to "female burnout" to "toxic day care," these so-called female crises have had their origins not in the actual conditions of women's lives but rather in a closed system that starts and ends in the media, popular culture, and advertising—an endless feedback loop that perpetuates and exaggerates its own false images of womanhood.

GUERRILLA GIRLS' POP QUIZ.

Q. If February is Black History Month and March is Women's History Month, what happens the rest of the year?

A. Discrimination.

www.guerrillagirls.com/posters/quiz.html. Reprinted with permission.

Women themselves don't single out the women's movement as the source of their misery. To the contrary, in national surveys 75 to 95 percent of women credit the feminist campaign with *improving* their lives, and a similar proportion say that the women's movement should keep pushing for change. Less than 8 percent think the women's movement might have actually made their lot worse. . . .

THE BACKLASH

Some women began to piece the picture together. In the 1989 *New York Times* poll, more than half of black women and one-fourth of white women put it into words. They told pollsters they believed men were now trying to retract the gains women had made in the last twenty years. "I wanted more autonomy," was how one woman, a thirty-seven-year-old nurse, put it. And her estranged husband "wanted to take it away."

The truth is that the last decade has seen a powerful counter-assault on women's rights, a backlash, an attempt to retract the handful of small and hard-won victories that the feminist movement did manage to win for women. This counterassault is largely insidious: in a kind of pop-culture version of the Big Lie, it stands the truth boldly on its head and proclaims that the very steps that have elevated women's position have actu-ally led to their downfall.

The backlash is at once sophisticated and banal, deceptively "progressive" and proudly backward. It deploys both the "new" findings of "scientific research" and the dime-store moralism of yesteryear; it turns into media sound bites both the glib pronouncements of pop-psych trend-watchers and the frenzied rhetoric of New Right preachers. The backlash has succeeded in framing virtually the whole issue of women's rights in its own language. Just as Reaganism shifted political discourse far to the right and demonized liberalism, so the backlash convinced the public that women's "liberation" was the true contemporary American scourge—the source of an endless laundry list of personal, social, and economic problems.

LOSING GROUND

But what has made women unhappy in the last decade is not their "equality"—which they don't yet have—but the rising pressure to halt, and even reverse, women's quest for that equal-ity. The "man shortage" and the "infertility epidemic" are not the price of liberation; in fact, they do not even exist. But these chimeras are the chisels of a society-wide backlash. They are part of a relentless whittling-down process—much of it amounting to outright propaganda—that has served to stir women's private anxieties and break their political wills. Iden-tifying feminism as women's enemy only furthers the ends of a backlash against women's equality, simultaneously deflecting attention from the backlash's central role and recruiting women to attack their own cause.

Some social observers may well ask whether the current

pressures on women actually constitute a backlash—or just a continuation of American society's long-standing resistance to women's rights. Certainly hostility to female independence has always been with us. But if fear and loathing of feminism is a sort of perpetual viral condition in our culture, it is not always in an acute stage; its symptoms subside and resurface periodically. And it is these episodes of resurgence, such as the one we face now, that can accurately be termed "backlashes" to women's advancement. If we trace these occurrences in American history, we find such flare-ups are hardly random; they have always been triggered by the perception—accurate or not—that women are making great strides. These outbreaks are backlashes because they have always arisen in reaction to women's "progress," caused not simply by a bedrock of misogyny but by the specific efforts of contemporary women to improve their status, efforts that have been interpreted time and again by men—especially men grappling with real threats to their economic and social well-being on other fronts—as spelling their own masculine doom.

DETERMINED OPPOSITION

The most recent round of backlash first surfaced in the late '70s on the fringes, among the evangelical right. By the early '80s, the fundamentalist ideology had shouldered its way into the White House. By the mid-'80s, as resistance to women's rights acquired political and social acceptability, it passed into the popular culture. And in every case, the timing coincided with signs that women were believed to be on the verge of breakthrough.

Just when women's quest for equal rights seemed closest to achieving its objectives, the backlash struck it down. Just when a "gender gap" at the voting booth surfaced in 1980, and women in politics began to talk of capitalizing on it, the Republican party elevated Ronald Reagan and both political parties began to shunt women's rights off their platforms. Just when support for feminism and the Equal Rights Amendment reached a record high in 1981, the amendment was defeated the following year. Just when women were starting to mobilize against battering and sexual assaults, the federal government stalled funding for battered-women's programs, defeated bills to fund shelters, and shut down its Office of Domestic Violence—only two years after opening it in 1979. Just when record numbers of younger women were supporting feminist goals in the mid-'80s (more of them, in fact, than older women) and a majority of all women were calling themselves feminists, the media declared the advent of a younger "postfeminist generation" that supposedly reviled the women's movement. Just when women racked up their largest percentage ever supporting the right to abortion, the U.S. Supreme Court moved toward reconsidering it.

In other words, the antifeminist backlash has been set off not by women's achievement of full equality but by the increased possibility that they might win it. It is a preemptive strike that stops women long before they reach the finish line. "A backlash may be an indication that women really have had an effect," feminist psychologist Dr. Jean Baker Miller has written, "but backlashes occur when advances have been small, before changes are sufficient to help many people. . . . It is almost as if the leaders of backlashes use the fear of change as a threat before major change has occurred.". . .

DEFENDING FEMINISM

To blame feminism for women's "lesser life" is to miss entirely the point of feminism, which is to win women a wider range of experience. Feminism remains a pretty simple concept, despite repeated—and enormously effective—efforts to dress it up in greasepaint and turn its proponents into gargoyles. As Rebecca West wrote sardonically in 1913, "I myself have never been able to find out precisely what feminism is: I only know that people call me a feminist whenever I express sentiments that differentiate me from a doormat."

The meaning of the word "feminist" has not really changed since it first appeared in a book review in the *Athenaeum* of April 27, 1895, describing a woman who "has in her the capacity of fighting her way back to independence." It is the basic proposition that, as Nora put it in Ibsen's *A Doll's House* a century ago, "Before everything else I'm a human being." It is the simply worded sign hoisted by a little girl in the 1970 Women's Strike for Equality: I AM NOT A BARBIE DOLL. Feminism asks the world to recognize at long last that women aren't decorative ornaments, worthy vessels, members of a "special-interest group." They are half (in fact, now more than half) of the national population, and just as deserving of rights and opportunities, just as capable of participating in the world's events, as the other half. Feminism's agenda is basic: It asks that women not be forced to "choose" between public justice and private happiness. It asks that women be free to define themselves—instead of having their identity defined for them, time and again, by their culture and their men.

The fact that these are still such incendiary notions should tell us that American women have a way to go before they enter the promised land of equality.

CHAPTER 3

THE THIRD WAVE AND THE FUTURE OF FEMINISM

AMERICAN
SOCIAL
MOVEMENTS

Keeping the
Movement Moving

Betty Friedan is one of the leading feminist figures of the twentieth century, and her book *The Feminine Mystique*, published in 1963,
is considered a classic feminist text. In the present selection, published
in the *New York Times Magazine* in 1985, Friedan argues that the feminist movement is in trouble. She believes that many feminist leaders have drifted away from the important issues that face middle-class
women in America. In particular, she believes that valuable energy
is being wasted on internal power struggles, that many feminists are
stuck in old ways of thinking, that younger people are not being
brought into the movement, and that many feminist organizations
are preoccupied with pornography and other sexual issues. Friedan
outlines ten things that she thinks ought to be done if the feminist
movement is to keep its momentum, and she concludes the article
by encouraging feminists to embrace a humanist perspective in
which women and men work together to improve the world and
the lives of everyone in it.

This is addressed to any woman who has ever said "we"
about the women's movement, including those who say,
"I'm not a feminist, but. . . ." And it's addressed to quite a few
men.

It's a personal message, not at all objective, and it's in response
to those who think our modern women's movement is over—
either because it is defeated and a failure, or because it has tri-
umphed, its work done, its mission accomplished. After all, any
daughter can now dream of being an astronaut, after Sally
Ride, or running for President, after Geraldine Ferraro.

I do not think that the job of the modern women's movement is done. And I do not believe the movement has failed. For one thing, those of us who started the modern women's movement, or came into it after marriage and children or from jobs as "invisible women" in the office, still carry the glow of "it changed my whole life," an aliveness, the satisfaction of finding our own voice and power, and the skills we didn't have a chance to develop before.

I do believe, though, that the movement is in trouble. I was too passionately involved in its conception, its birth, its growing pains, its youthful flowering, to acquiesce quietly to its going gently so soon into the night. But, like a lot of other mothers, I have been denying the symptoms of what I now feel forced to confront as a profound paralysis of the women's movement in America. And this, in turn, has forced me to think about how we can get the women's movement moving again—a new round of consciousness-raising, for instance, or utilizing the networks of professional women, or ceasing the obsession with the matter of pornography.

A Movement in Trouble

I see as symptoms of the paralysis the impotence in the face of fundamentalist backlash; the wasting of energy in internal power struggles when no real issues are at stake; the nostalgic harking back to old rhetoric, old ideas, old modes of action instead of confronting new threats and new problems with new thinking; the failure to mobilize the young generation who take for granted the rights we won and who do not defend those rights as they are being taken away in front of our eyes, and the preoccupation with pornography and other sexual diversions that do not affect most women's lives. I sense an unwillingness to deal with the complex realities of female survival in male-modeled careers, with the new illusions of having it all in marriage and equality in divorce, and with the basic causes of the grim feminization of poverty. The potential of women's political power is slipping away between the poles of self-serving feminist illusion and male and female opportunism.

The promise of that empowerment of women that enabled so many of us to change our own lives is being betrayed by our failure to mobilize the next generation to move beyond us....

How can we let the women's movement die out here in America when what we began is taking hold now all over the world? I would like to suggest 10 things that might be done to break the blocks that seem to have stymied the women's movement in America:

SOLUTIONS FOR THE FUTURE

1. Begin a new round of consciousness raising for the new generation. These women, each thinking she is alone with her personal guilt and pressures, trying to "have it all," having second thoughts about her professional career, desperately trying to have a baby before it is too late, with or without husband, and maybe secretly blaming the movement for getting her into this mess, are almost as isolated, and as powerless in their isolation, as those suburban housewives afflicted by "the problem that had no name" whom I interviewed for "The Feminine Mystique" over 20 years ago. Those women put a name to their problem; they got together with other women in the new feminist groups and began to work for political solutions and began to change their lives.

That has to happen again to free a new generation of women from its new double burden of guilt and isolation. The guilts of less-than-perfect motherhood and less-than-perfect professional career performance are real because it's not possible to "have it all" when jobs are still structured for men whose wives take care of the details of life, and homes are still structured for women whose only responsibility is running their families. I warned five years ago that if the women's movement didn't move into a second stage and take on the problems of restructuring work and home, a new generation would be vulnerable to backlash. But the movement has not moved into that needed second stage, so the women struggling with these new problems view them as purely personal, not political, and no longer look to the movement for solutions.

Putting new names to their problems, they might stop feeling guilty for not being able to conduct their professional lives just like men, might give each other support in new patterns of professional advance and parenting, might together demand new political solutions of parental leave and child care from company or profession or community, or even, once again, from government. They might, then, find new energy to save the rights they now take for granted or even secretly resent, because they are so hard to live with. 2. Mobilize the new professional networks and the old established volunteer organizations to save women's rights. We can't fight fundamentalist backlash with backward-looking feminist fundamentalism. Second-stage feminism is itself pluralistic, and has to use new pluralist strengths and strategies. The women who have been 30 and 40 percent of the graduating class from law school or business school and 47 percent of the journalism school classes, the ones who've taken women's studies, the women who grew up playing Little League baseball and cheered on those new champion women athletes, the new professional networks of women in every field, every woman who has been looking to those networks only to get ahead in her own field, must now use her professional skills to save the laws and executive orders against sex discrimination in education and employment. They must restore the enforcement machinery and the class-action suits that opened up all these opportunities to her in the first place. . . .

FORGET ABOUT PORNOGRAPHY

3. Get off the pornography kick and face the real obscenity of poverty. No matter how repulsive we may find pornography, laws banning books or movies for sexually explicit content could be far more dangerous to women. The pornography issue is dividing the women's movement and giving the impression on college campuses that to be a feminist is to be against sex. More important, it is diverting energies that need to be spent saving the basic rights now being destroyed.

Karen DeCrow, who once was elected president of NOW

[National Organization for Women] on the slogan "Out of the mainstream, into the revolution," wrote a recent article entitled "Strange Bedfellows" for *Penthouse*. She pointed out that the new feminist-supported proposals to make pornography an illegal violation of the civil rights of women have an unlooked-for effect. They aid the far right agenda that would also ban the teaching of evolution in schools, prohibit a woman's right to choose abortion, cut Government funding for textbooks that portray women in nontraditional roles, and repeal Federal statutes against spouse and child abuse.

What is behind some women's obsession with pornography? Women's sexuality has been distorted and suppressed in almost every society, and that suppression has gone hand in hand with a general attempt to deny women freedom to control their own lives, to move and earn independently in society. Pornography, and also the crusade to suppress pornography, reduce women to a single dimension, defining them as only passive sex objects, not people who can run their own lives.

But I think the secret this obsession with pornography may mask for women alone, for aging women, and for women still more economically dependent on men than they would like, is fear of poverty, which is the ultimate obscenity for Americans. I sat at a dinner table recently with several women, who I know are struggling personally with these problems, and could not believe their venom against the young rock star Madonna. I suggested that teen-agers identified with her gutsiness, strength and independence as well as with her not-at-all-passive sexuality, which to me was not a retreat from women's liberation, but a celebration of it. Whoever said that feminism shouldn't be sexy!

They were women in their 40's, 50's and 60's, and they virtually spat in disgust. Perhaps an unspoken reason so many women are protesting sexually explicit materials is that their own sexuality is denied by society. But I suspect that as long as sex is distorted by women's economic dependence, or fear of it, it can't be truly, freely enjoyed. The obscenity that not even many feminists want to confront in personal terms is the sheer degradation of being poor in opulent, upwardly mobile America. Of course, the women's movement in America, like all such revolutions everywhere, has been mainly a middle-class movement, but the shameful secret it has never really dealt with is the fact that more and more middle-class women are sinking into poverty.

America's first movement for women's rights died out after winning the vote, four generations ago, because women didn't tackle the hard political tasks of restructuring home and work so that women who married and had children could also earn and have their own voice in the decision-making mainstream of society. Instead, those women retreated behind a cultural curtain of female "purity," focusing their energies on issues like prohibition, much like the pornographic obsession of some feminists today.

UNFAIR DIVORCES

4. Confront the illusion of equality in divorce. Economists and feminists have been talking a lot lately about "the feminization of poverty" in theoretical terms, but the American women's movement has not developed concrete strategies that get at its root cause. It's not just a question of women earning less than men—though as long as women do not get equal pay for work of comparable value, or earn Social Security or pensions for taking care of children and home, they are both economically dependent on marriage and motherhood and pay a big economic price for it. And this is as true for divorced aging yuppies as for welfare mothers.

A startling new book by the sociologist Lenore J. Weitzman, "The Divorce Revolution: The Unexpected Social and Economic Consequences for Women and Children in America," reveals that in the 1970's, when 48 states adopted "no-fault" divorce laws treating men and women "equally" in divorce settlements—laws feminists originally supported— divorced women and their children suffered an immediate 73 percent drop in their standard of living, while their ex-husbands enjoyed a 42 percent rise in theirs.

In dividing "marital property," Lenore Weitzman reports, judges have systematically overlooked the major assets of many marriages—the husband's career assets that the wife helped make possible, his professional education that she may have helped support, the career on which he was able to concentrate because she ran the home, and his salary, pension, health insurance and earning power that resulted. They have also ignored the wife's years of unpaid housework and child care (not totally insured by Social Security in the event of divorce) and her drastically diminished job prospects after divorce. And, for most, the "equal" division of property means the forced sale of the family home—which used to be awarded to the wife and children. Child support, which has often been inadequate, unpaid and uncollectable, usually ends when the child is 18, just as college expenses begin. Thus the vicious cycle whereby an ever-increasing majority of the truly poor in America are families headed by women.

A new generation of feminist lawyers and judges has now drafted, and must get urgent grass-roots political support for, the kind of law needed, a law that treats marriage as a true economic partnership—and includes fairer standards of property division, maintenance and child support. It should be a law that does not penalize women who have chosen family over, or even together with, professional career.

Choice in Abortions

5. Return the issue of abortion to the matter of women's own responsible choice. I think feminists have been so traumatized by the fundamentalist crusade against abortion and all the talk of fetuses and when life begins that they are in danger of forgetting the values that made abortion a feminist issue in the first place. Underneath the hysteria, poll after poll shows that the great majority of women in this nation, and most men, still want to decide when and whether to have a child in accordance with their own conscience. This includes women of faith, including the majority of Catholic women. Attacks on

the Pope and picketing the churches, as some desperate or deranged male and female abortion champions have lately proposed, would play right into the hands of our "right to life" enemies, who love to paint feminists as satanic opponents of God and family. We must not surrender family values and religious principles to the far right. Let the new women theologians and feminist women of faith in every church take on the fundamentalist preachers.

*"Our female employees are only making 70% of the men's wages . . .
better assign them more overtime."*

Simpson. © 1998, Carol Simpson. Reprinted with permission.

I think women who are young, and those not so young, today must be able to choose when to have a child, given the necessities of their jobs. They will indeed join their mothers, who remember the humiliations and dangers of back-street butcher abortions, in a march of millions to save the right of legal abortion. I certainly support a march for women's choice of birth control and legal abortion. NOW has called for one in the spring of 1986. 6. Affirm the differences between men and women. New feminist thinking is required if American women are to continue advancing in man's world, as they must, to earn their way, and yet "not become like men." This fear is heard with more and more frequency today from young women, including many who have succeeded, and some who have failed or opted out of male-defined careers. More books like Carol Gilligan's "In a Different Voice" and consciousness-raising sessions are needed. First-stage feminism denied real differences between women and men except for the sexual organs themselves. Some feminists still do not understand that true equality is not possible unless those differences between men and women are affirmed and until values based on female sensitivities to life begin to be voiced in every discipline and profession, from architecture to economics, where, until recently, all concepts and standards were defined by men. This is not a matter of abstract theory alone but involves the restructuring of hours of work and patterns of professional training so that they take into account the fact that women are the people who give birth to children. It must lead to concrete changes in medical practice, church worship, the writing of history, standards of ethics, even the design of homes and appliances. 7. Breakthrough for older women. The women's movement has never put serious energy into the job that must be done to get women adequately covered by Social Security and pensions, especially those women now reaching 65 who spent many years as housewives and are ending up alone. The need for more independent and shared housing for older women now living alone in suburban houses they can't afford to sell, or lonely furnished rooms—and the need for services and jobs or volunteer options that will enable them to keep on living independent, productive lives—has never been a part of the women's movement agenda. But that first generation of feminist mothers, women now in their 60's, is a powerful political resource for the movement as these women retire from late or early professional or volunteer careers. Women in their 50's and 60's are shown by the polls to be more firmly committed than their daughters to the feminist goals of equality. Let the women's movement lead the rest of society in breaking the spell of the youth cult and drawing on the still enormous energies and the wisdom that may come to some of us in age.

MAKING ROOM FOR MEN

8. Bring in the men. It's passe, surely, for feminists now to see men only as the enemy, or to contemplate separatist models for emotional or economic survival. Feminist theorists like Barbara Ehrenreich cite dismal evidence of the "new men" opting out of family responsibilities altogether. But in my own life I seem to see more and more young men, and older ones—even former male chauvinist pigs—admitting their vulnerability and learning to express their tenderness, sharing the care of the kids, even though most of them may never share it equally with their wives.

And as men let down their masks of machismo, and admit their dependence on the women in their lives, women may admit a new need to depend on men, without fear of sinking back into the old abject subservience. After all, even women who insist they are not, and never will be, feminists have learned to defend themselves against real male brutality. Look at Charlotte Donahue Fedders, the wife of that Security and Exchange commissioner, who testified in divorce court about his repeated abuse—his repeated beatings caused black eyes and a broken eardrum. At one time, a woman in her situation would have kept that shame a secret. The Reagan Administration had to ask him to resign, because wife-beating is no longer politically acceptable, even in conservative America in 1985.

I don't think women can, or should try to, take the responsibility for liberating men from the remnants of machismo. But there has to be a new way of asking what do men really want, to echo Freud, a new kind of dialogue that breaks through or gets behind both our masks. Women cannot restructure jobs or homes just by talking to themselves. 9. Continue to fight for real political power. Although feminists do not now, and never really did, support a woman just because she is a woman, there is no substitute for having women in political offices that matter. But more women are discovering that they have to fight, as men do, in primaries where victory is not certain, and not just wait for an "open seat." After the E.R.A.'s defeat, feminists and their supporters raised money nationally to run women candidates in virtually every district in Illinois, Florida and North Carolina where legislators voted against the amendment. And in that single election they increased sizably women's representation in those state legislatures. 10. MOVE BEYOND SINGLE-issue thinking. Even today, I do not think women's rights are the most urgent business for American women. The important thing is somehow getting together with men who also put the values of life first to break through the paralysis that fundamentalist backlash has imposed on all our movements. It is not only feminism that is becoming a dirty word in America, but also liberalism, humanism, pluralism, environmentalism and civil liberties. The very freedom of political dissent that enabled the women's movement to start here has been made to seem unsafe for today's young men as well as young women. I think the yuppies are afraid to be political.

Women may have to think beyond "women's issues" to join their energies with men to redeem our democratic tradition and turn our nation's power to the interests of life instead of the nuclear arms race that is paralyzing it. I've never, for instance, seen the need for a separate women's peace movement. I'm not really sure that women, by nature, are more peace-loving than men. They were simply not brought up to express aggression the way men do (they took it out covertly, on themselves and on their men and children, psychologists would say). But the human race may not survive much longer unless women move beyond the nurture of their own babies and careers to political decisions of war and peace, and unless men who share the nurture of their children take responsibility for ending the arms race before it destroys all life. In that sense, I think the women's movement is only a particular moment in human evolution, and once its job is really done, then it can and should be allowed to fade away, honorably discharged.

White Women's Feminism

VERONICA CHAMBERS

In this piece, Veronica Chambers, an author and general editor at *Newsweek*, discusses black women and feminism. In her opinion, much contemporary feminism is dominated by white women and white perspectives, and specific issues that black women face tend to be excluded. As a young black feminist, Chambers says, she often encounters racism from white feminists, and she seldom feels truly welcome or appreciated at feminist gatherings. Furthermore, Chambers says, she cannot feel at home in any movement that refuses to recognize that some men, in particular black men in America, are also victims of oppression and discrimination. Black women, Chambers believes, might not have much to gain from participating in the women's movement, at least in the mainstream, mostly white, women's movement. Rather, she suggests, it may perhaps be more fruitful for black women to work within their own cultural frameworks to bring about change.

It was a sinking feeling in the pit of my gut. Not anger really, but disappointment. I am talking about the first time feminism broke my heart. I was a college student in the late eighties, espousing feminism with the fervor and delight with which I had espoused black studies. Being black and female all my life, I had felt a double invisibility, like the double veil that W.E.B. Du Bois wrote about in *The Souls of Black Folk*. When I discovered black studies and women's studies, I felt that I had learned to speak all over again. There was a context for my particular existence. A vocabulary for my situation. An agenda to empower myself and others.

Little did I know that women's studies and black studies were not too different from those old water faucets where both hot water and cold water run, but never shall the two meet. Growing up in the black community, I knew that sexism often accompanied an Afrocentric perspective. What I was not ready for was the racism of white women, women who called themselves progressive, liberal, even radical. And when the trust I put in these women—and in what increasingly felt like *their* movement—was betrayed, I felt hurt and confused. It would not be the last time.

Recently I went to the library to research black women feminists. I typed the words "African American," "women" and "feminists" into the reference computer. The machine searched all the recent magazine articles that included all three words. I found three articles—two by bell hooks, one by Rebecca Walker. It's not that there aren't black feminists, but the journals and periodicals that they appear in tend to be small and underfunded and don't make it into the *Reader's Guide* database. In larger and more mainstream media, coverage for and about feminists too often focuses on white women feminists. As a result, the presence of black women has been all but erased by the media and, in turn, the history books.

CHOOSING SIDES

To be a young, black feminist today, I believe, is to feel unsure that your needs and interests can be fully addressed in any one camp. It seems that for sanity's sake you must choose sides—your skin color versus your gender, blacks (implicitly male) versus women (implicitly white). Because of the pressing problems in the community—poverty, drugs, men's absence from many of our families—most young black women choose to play the game like boys on a b-ball court. When it comes down to picking teams—skins vs. shirts—most of us opt to play skin, shedding our gender questions like a layer of clothing that becomes tedious and superfluous on a hot ghetto day.

As rapper Heavy D. put it, "Picking cotton was hard, but we

picked it together." In the United States, in 1995, black women and black men are not together—in our families or in our communities. This is something that white women often fail to understand—that for us, unifying the community is of paramount importance. Our struggle is not just with the black male "patriarchy"; it is often more complicated than that. In this society, black men are increasingly powerless and too often believe themselves to be powerless. Too many of them take their anger out on the only people they feel are within their domain—"their" women and children. It is wrong. It is unfair. And it is frightening. But it is also pitiful.

BLACK MEN SUFFERING

I have seen the look in my father's eyes after he has been pulled over by the police for driving what they deemed a "pimp-mobile," a Lincoln Continental. I have watched my brother be transformed from a kid who loved cartoons and video games to a boy 'n the hood, a so-called menace to society. But I have also watched him come home and hang his head in shame because he has no money, he has no high school diploma and he has a police record. He is twenty-one years old and he already acts like a broken man. I have looked into the eyes of lovers and friends and seen fear, disappointment and weakness. I have sat on the subway and watched old black men, my grandfather's age, sing and dance, cup in hand, like Sambo or a modern-day minstrel show. I've watched white people clap and smile and oblige with spare change, seemingly unaware of how degrading it is for a seventy-year-old black man to sing 1920s ditties for his supper. I believe in the African traditions of ancestral worship and elder-run societies. Every time I see an old black man beg, my heart is heavy with pain. These are my brothers and my father figures—any feminism that I embrace must be humanist enough to recognize that they have also been wronged.

Seven years ago I went to Simon's Rock College, a good liberal arts, liberal politics school in western Massachusetts. Like many young women of all colors and ethnic backgrounds, I had my first feminist awakening at college. Through books and classes and a dynamic women's studies teacher, Dr. Patricia Sharpe, I found Simone de Beauvoir and Gloria Steinem, Alice Walker and Paula Gunn Allen. My first year, Barbara Smith gave a lecture, and for me, she was like a silver-screen apparition. Black *and* feminist—a rare bird that I'd only read about and never actually seen.

WOMEN WITH STRENGTH

I come from a family of strong black women, but to my mother, feminism was a four-letter word. To the people in my neighborhood, feminists were man-haters. Feminists were also referred to as lesbians—a stigmatized status, given the rampant homophobia in the black community. To be strong, smart, independent and *unashamed* were necessary elements for survival in the Brooklyn of my youth. The black women I knew growing up embodied these qualities with the wiles and grace of Amazon warriors. They were, in other words, sisters who didn't take no shit. I knew strength, and I was taught from birth, "Don't allow no man to walk all over you." My mother, once a battered wife, had lived many years in fear and gave me strength as my most valuable inheritance. She had a small but potent circle of women friends who could count on each other for sustenance, both physical and emotional; who encouraged each other to keep on keepin' on; who were good for advice and for actual physical help—if you needed to move, if you needed someone to watch the kids, if you needed to know how to deal with your creep of a boss at work.

When I bought Barbara Smith's *Home Girls: A Black Feminist Anthology,* I carried it like a prayer book. It was in this book that I first read Audre Lorde, Michelle Cliff, June Jordan and Luisah Teish. When I read Michelle Cliff's "If I Could Write This in Fire, I Would Write This in Fire," the title alone reverberated in my head like a drumbeat. As I continued my readings, I realized that in all incarnations of the women's movement, black women were there. At the turn of the century, there were black women who were both abolitionists and

A Condescending Attitude Toward Black Women

The understanding I had by age thirteen of patriarchal politics created in me expectations of the feminist movement that were quite different from those of young, middle class, white women. When I entered my first women's studies class at Stanford University in the early 1970s, white women were reveling in the joy of being together—to them it was an important, momentous occasion. I had not known a life where women had not been together, where women had not helped, protected, and loved one another deeply. I had not known white women who were ignorant of the impact of race and class on their social status and consciousness (Southern white women often have a more realistic perspective on racism and classism than white women in other areas of the United States.) I did not feel sympathetic to white peers who maintained that I could not expect them to have knowledge of or understand the life experiences of black women. Despite my

suffragists. There were black women in the sixties and seventies giving their time and effort to the struggle, demanding that white men and white women take them seriously. When white women talked about equality, we insisted that they mean black women too. But as it was, at any table of discussion our specific issues were—and still often are—low on the list of priorities. Even among feminists, we are "minorities." That simply isn't good enough.

THE INFLUENCE OF RACE

White feminists of earlier generations have passed these values onto their daughters. The young women I went to school with, for all their notions of feminism, still basked in the glory and background (living in racially segregated communities) I knew about the lives of white women, and certainly no white women lived in our neighborhood, attended our schools, or worked in our homes.

When I participated in feminist groups, I found that white women adopted a condescending attitude towards me and other non-white participants. The condescension they directed at black women was one of the means they employed to remind us that the women's movement was "theirs"—that we were able to participate because they allowed it, even encouraged it; after all, we were needed to legitimate the process. They did not see us as equals. They did not treat us as equals.... If we dared to criticize the movement or to assume responsibility for reshaping feminist ideas and introducing new ideas, our voices were tuned out, dismissed, silenced. We could be heard only if our statements echoed the sentiments of the dominant discourse.

bell hooks, "Black Women: Shaping Feminist Theory," in *Feminist Theory: From Margin to Center*, pp. 11–12.

privilege of their whiteness. I remember being very upset during a first-year English class because on the day when we were supposed to have read a Toni Cade Bambara story, no one in the class had read it except me. The white boys I dismissed more readily—I knew they didn't care. But the white girls, the same ones who would proclaim their sisterhood time after time, had simply been too lazy or too uninterested to read the only story by a black woman on our syllabus. Was it racist? No, of course not. But it was insensitive and myopic, and I was furious. Hadn't I read Willa Cather? Hadn't I dived right into Margaret Atwood? Hadn't I explored worlds foreign to my own? I guess that was why I had been so excited to read the Toni Cade Bambara story. I wanted the class to know what my world was like, what our parties were like, what my people were like. It seemed nobody, including the white women, cared.

My junior year, I was awarded a women's studies scholarship to complement the "minority" scholarship that had enabled me to attend this expensive college in the first place. Outside of class, I became active in both "minority" student groups and the wimmin's center. Often at the wimmin's center, I'd be one of only a handful of women of color. I tried to persuade my black friends to come, but they just weren't interested. Little by little, I became frustrated with being the token black at the women's activities. Like many black women before me, I learned the hard way that some people, including many white feminists, like having blacks at their meetings and social gatherings. Whether you were happy there, whether you were taken seriously there, was beside the point. To have a black presence was and is trendy. It is politically correct. But when it came down to it, I could not trust most white women to have my back.

OBSTACLES FOR BLACK FEMINISTS

Every couple of months, one or another of the glossy women's magazines runs an article about shoplifting. Take, for example, an article entitled "The Thrill of the Steal" by Kathryn Harrison that appeared in *Mademoiselle* in October of 1993. Like many of these pieces, this one suggests that a lot of women shoplift as an act of female aggression against the big, bad male system of capitalism. "The stores from which women steal," Harrison writes, "together with the apparatus for detection and apprehension, are often experienced as masculine and patriarchal worlds."

What Harrison doesn't say is that those are essentially white patriarchal worlds. If shoplifting can be construed as a feminist act, then whose feminist act is it? My black female friends could never take such a "feminist" stand because *we* would be caught. We are tailed in every store we enter, from Kmart to Bloomingdales to Saks Fifth Avenue. We are harassed and assumed to be "browsing"/ "shoplifting" wherever we go. My friends Sarah and Renée, on the other hand, card-carrying feminists that they are, are habitual shoplifters. It is "getting even," Sarah says with glee, mailing me a copy of the *Mademoiselle* article. No wonder black women sometimes feel that they have no time for white women. Sisterhood, sometimes, is simply trifling.

Another major obstacle among feminists of my generation is how black women are still expected to fit white standards of beauty and how little white women acknowledge or understand this. While white women are also held to unreasonable beauty standards, it is frustrating how often many women try to skirt around the reality that racism adds another potent strain to the standards of beauty that black women are held to. To say simply, "I don't look like Cindy Crawford either," or "I think Whitney Houston is *really* beautiful," doesn't address the real pain that many black women have experienced. We are still acculturated to hate our dark skin, our kinky hair, our full figures. "What are you going to do? You can't dye your skin," African American model Veronica Webb said in a recent interview. What are you gonna do? You're not gonna talk to your white sisters because they're so busy being defensive, so busy assuring you that they aren't racist, that they rarely hear what you're saying at all.

A DISAPPOINTING BETRAYAL

It was with this feeling of disappointment and betrayal that I read Naomi Wolf's *The Beauty Myth*. Surely, Wolf would address how the tyranny of the beauty myth had scarred so many women of color—not only black women, but Asian, Latina and American Indian women as well. She did not. And as far as I could tell, in all of the media hoopla that surrounded her, neither the white press nor the black press called her on it. Furthermore, Wolf made the classic mistake of positing blacks versus women as if six percent of the population—millions of women—were not both. "A black employee can now charge, sympathetically, that he doesn't *want* to look more white, and should not have to look more white in order to keep his job," writes Wolf. "Though the professional beauty qualification ranks women in a similar biological caste system, female identity is not yet recognized to be remotely as legitimate as racial identity (faintly though that is recognized)." Notice that Wolf uses the generic "he" when she refers to a black employee. Moreover, by implying that blacks are somehow ahead of women in terms of cultural legitimacy, Wolf fails to recognize that for black women, by the very nature of their womanhood, this cannot be true. As for the rigidity of corporate society, Wolf does not even give voice to the many ways that black women *are* instructed to look as "white" as possible, especially with regard to their hair. She doesn't mention the African American flight attendant who brought a famous suit against her employers, who had fired her because she wore braids. She doesn't mention how often braids, dreads and even Afros are strictly prohibited in many workplaces, forcing many black women to straighten their hair and wear styles that are more "mainstream." In a book full of figures and facts and well-documented research, Wolf committed a classic act of betrayal feminism. Maybe she did not know about the issues that face black women and other women of color. But she should have made it her business to find out.

DIVERGING PATHS

It is this sense of invisibility and betrayal that makes many young feminists of color think that the idea of a women's movement may not necessarily serve their best interests. Better, some contend, to work within your cultural and multicultural frameworks to infuse the men with a broader ideology. I stand on the shoulders of women like Barbara Smith, Audre Lorde and Luisah Teish, but I suffer as they did from a numbing isolation. I cannot change the mind of every white feminist that I encounter. That is not my interest or my job. Unfortunately, within white women's organizations, what little female solidarity I feel is overshadowed by a much greater sense of tokenism, racism, ignorance and condescension. I continue with my work because I know that eventually something must give.

But looking at how far we have come since the sixties and seventies shows that among women, racism remains too big a beast for black women to conquer alone. White women must look within themselves and their organizations and address the issue of why more women of color do not stand by their side. Only then will we be any closer to truly being sisters.

Ecofeminism

CAROL J. ADAMS

In this piece, Carol J. Adams, the author of several books on animal
rights and feminism, argues that there is an important connection
between the oppression of women and the exploitation of the natural world. Adams argues that just as fundamental rights were
wrongly denied to women, they are today wrongly denied to animals. Feminism, she believes, can help people recognize that such activities as eating meat, wearing fur, and using animals for research are
wrong. Furthermore, she argues, because feminists are accustomed
to critically examining human interactions, they are well positioned
to use these skills to examine how human beings interact with the
nonhuman world. Adams considers and rejects various arguments
for the view that feminism and animal rights are at odds with one
another, and argues that the world would be much better for human
beings if animal exploitation were to end.

Feminists, building on women's experiences, have empha-
sized such values as connectedness, responsibility, attentive
love, an embodied ethic incorporating body-mediated knowledge. If we were to touch, hear, and see animals whom we eat,
wear, or otherwise use, we might replace current exploitation
with a respectful relationship.

Notions of human nature exaggerate differences and min-
imize similarities between the other animals and ourselves. We
talk about animals as if we were not animals ourselves. This
permits humans in the United States alone to imprison almost
six billion animals in intensive farming systems that violate the
animals' basic physical and behavioral needs; to tolerate the
killing of as many as three animals a second in laboratories; to
purchase fur garments that require the suffering and death of

at least 70 million animals each year; to hunt and kill 200 million animals annually for "sport"; and to exhibit millions of animals in circuses, rodeos, and zoos, where they endure boredom, mistreatment, lack of privacy, and deprivation of their natural environment.

Noticing Similarities

Parallels between women's experiences and those of other animals have been made repeatedly in feminist literature and theory. Animals are meat, experimental guinea pigs, and objectified bodies; women are treated like meat, guinea pigs, and objectified bodies. We see pornographic pictures of "beaver hunters" who "bag" a woman, or of women put through meat grinders. Batterers have forced their victims to watch the killing of a favorite animal. Sexually abused children are sometimes threatened with a pet's death to ensure their compliance. "Why Can't This Veal Calf Walk?" by performance artist Karen Finley is a poem about rape and incest. (Well, why can't she or he walk? Kept in small crates, "veal" calves are unable to turn around, since exercise would increase muscle development, toughen the flesh, and slow weight gain. Standing on slatted floors causes a constant strain. Diarrhea, resulting from an improper diet that fosters anemia to produce pale flesh, causes the slats to become slippery; the calves often fall, getting leg injuries. When taken to be slaughtered, many can hardly walk.)

Raised in enclosed, darkened, or dimly lit buildings, other intensively farmed animals fare as poorly, their lives characterized by little extraneous stimuli, restricted movement, no freedom to choose social interactions, intense and unpleasant fumes, and ingestion of subtherapeutic doses of antibiotics (50 percent of the antibiotics in the U.S. go to livestock). Hens are kept as many as five to a cage with dimensions only slightly larger than this magazine. When being cooked in an oven, the chicken has four times more space than when she was alive.

Many feminists have noted that women's oppression and animal exploitation are interrelated. Rosemary Ruether has established a connection between the domestication of animals, the development of urban centers, the creation of slavery, and the inequality of the sexes. Some anthropologists correlate male domination with hunting economies. One ecofeminist, Sally Abbott, speculates that patriarchal religion resulted from the guilt of consuming animals. Another, Elizabeth Fisher, proposes that the breeding of animals suggested ways to control women's reproductivity. Gena Corea shows how embryo transfer was applied to women after being developed in the cattle industry. Andrée Collard and others argue that the beast slain in hero mythologies represents the once powerful goddess.

Feminist philosophers have exposed the methodology of science as arising from and valorizing human male (usually white, heterosexual, and upper-class) experience. They say that how science defines or selects research problems, how it defines *why* these are problems, how it designs experiments, constructs and confers meaning—all aspects of science also used to defend animal experimentation—are sexist, racist, homophobic, and classist. Animal rights adds speciesism to this analysis.

Yet for many, feminism and animal rights are antithetical, partly because of approaches adopted by the animal rights movement. Who isn't offended by a poster of a woman that declares, "It takes up to 40 dumb animals to make a fur coat. But only one to wear it."? Why have farm animals—who represent at least 90 percent of the exploited animals—not been the focus of animal activism, rather than such women-identified consumer objects as cosmetics and furs? No law requires the testing of cosmetics on animals, and so, like fur, cosmetics are equated with vanity, and are seen as more expendable than animal foods. Furthermore, women are seen as more caring about animals. The animal rights movement seems to sense that women will identify with the exploited animal because of our own exploitation.

Some feminists fear that animal rights would set a precedent for the rights of fetuses. Ironically, antiabortionists agree, assailing activists for caring about animals but not fetuses. But it is disingenuous to compare a fetus with a living, breathing animal. A fetus has potential interests; an animal has actual interests. Speciesism is perhaps nowhere more pronounced than in the protestation about the fate of the human conceptus, while the sentience of other animals is declared morally irrelevant because they are not human. Some antiabortionists define meaningful life so broadly as to encompass a newly fertilized egg, yet so narrowly that fully grown animals with well-developed nervous systems and social sensibilities are excluded. Extending the feminist understanding of reproductive freedom, we see that both women and other female animals experience enforced pregnancies.

ANIMAL PRODUCTION WASTES RESOURCES

Animal rights is charged with being antihuman. (This is reminiscent of "antimen" charges against feminists.) It is convenient to divide the issue of animal rights from human rights issues, to complain that we are concerned about animals when humans are starving. But this division is perpetuated out of ignorance; animal agriculture greatly *contributes* to the devastation of the environment and to inequity in food distribution. Frances Moore Lappé describes how half of all water consumed in the United States, much of it from unrenewable resources, is used for crops fed to livestock. More than 50 percent of water pollution is due to wastes from the livestock industry (including manure, eroded soil, and synthetic pesticides and fertilizers). "Meat" production also places demands on energy sources: the 500 calories of food energy from one pound of cooked "steak" requires 20,000 calories of fossil fuel. Some environmentalists argue that 40 percent of our imported oil requirements would be cut if we switched to a vegetarian diet (because of the energy used in growing food for animals, keeping them alive, killing them, and processing their bodies). Livestock are responsible for 85 percent of topsoil erosion, and methane gas, much of it being emitted by cows being raised to be our food, accounts for at least 20 percent of the human contribution to the greenhouse effect.

Actually, animal *exploitation* is antihuman. In positing animal suffering as essential to human progress and conceptualizing morality so that this suffering is deemed irrelevant, a deformed definition of humanity prevails. Besides environmental degradation, many human illnesses are linked to eating animals (on a pure vegetarian diet the risk of death by heart attack is reduced from 50 percent to 4 percent, and the risk of breast and ovarian cancer is three times lower). Animal research now wastes billions of tax dollars yielding misleading results because it fails to use models that could produce information more quickly, more reliably, and for less cost than animal "models."

A Personal Change

Charges that animal rights is antihuman really mean: "The animal rights movement is against what I am doing and so is against me." If animal rights arguments are persuasive, personal change becomes necessary. As with feminism, if you accept the arguments, the consequences are immediate. You can't go on living the way you have, for suddenly you understand your complicity with an immense amount of exploitation. This can be very discomforting if you enjoy eating or wearing dead animals, or accept the premises of animal experimentation.

I know: that described me. For the first half of my life I ate animals and benefited in other ways from their exploitation. But feminism predisposed me to wonder if this was right or necessary. It equipped me to challenge language that removes agency and cloaks violence: "Someone kills animals so I can eat their corpses as meat" becomes "animals are killed to be eaten as meat," then "animals are meat," and finally "meat animals," thus "meat." Something *we do to animals* has become instead something that is a part of animals' nature, and we lose consideration of our role entirely. Alice Walker regained understanding of this role through a horse, recalling that "human animals and nonhuman animals can communicate quite well," and perceiving in eating "steak," "I am eating misery."

If the model for humanity was, say, a vegetarian feminist, rather than a male meat eater, our idea of human nature would be fundamentally challenged—animals would be seen as kin, not as prey, "models," or "animal machines"; *we* would be seen as radically in relationship with these kin, not as predators, experimenters, or owners. Reconstructing human nature as feminists includes examining how we as humans interact with the nonhuman world. Animal rights is not antihuman; it is antipatriarchal.

The Class Ceiling

Barbara Ehrenreich is a journalist, public speaker, and the author of numerous books. In this piece, she argues that growing class differences threaten to destroy the feminist movement. According to Ehrenreich, in the early stages of feminism most women were united through common duties of housecleaning, child care, shopping, and cooking. Although there were class differences, she notes, women tended to see themselves as sharing a common position in society as women. Today, she says, with women engaging in more diverse careers, frequent-flying female executives often see themselves as having little in common with working-class women. Oddly enough, Ehrenreich believes, feminism has helped increase class differences among women and the result, she argues, is that many core feminist issues are being neglected. Ehrenreich believes that if feminism is to survive, it has to return to its egalitarian roots and address class inequality.

Here's a scene from feminist ancient history: It's 1972 and about 20 of us are gathered in somebody's living room for our weekly "women's support group" meeting. We're all associated, in one way or another, with a small public college catering mostly to "nontraditional" students, meaning those who are older, poorer and more likely to be black or Latina than typical college students in this suburban area. Almost every level of the college hierarchy is represented—students of all ages, clerical workers, junior faculty members and even one or two full professors. There are acknowledged differences among us—race and sexual preference, for example—which we examine eagerly and a little anxiously. But we are comfortable together, and excited to have a chance to discuss

From "Doing It for Ourselves: Can Feminism Survive Class Polarization?" by Barbara Ehrenreich, *In These Times*, November 28, 1999. Copyright © 1999 by *In These Times*. Reprinted with permission.

152 • THE FEMINIST MOVEMENT

everything from the administration's sexist policies to our personal struggles with husbands and lovers. Whatever may divide us, we are all women, and we understand this to be one of the great defining qualities of our lives and politics.

Could a group so diverse happily convene today [1999]? Please let me know if you can offer a present day parallel, but I tend to suspect the answer is "very seldom" or "not at all." Perhaps the biggest social and economic trend of the past three decades has been class polarization—the expanding inequality in income and wealth. As United for a Fair Economy's excellent book, *Shifting Fortunes: The Perils of the Growing American Wealth Gap*, points out, the most glaring polarization has occurred between those at the very top of the income distribution—the upper 1 to 5 percent—and those who occupy the bottom 30 to 40 percent. Less striking, but more ominous for the future of feminism, is the growing gap between those in the top 40 percent and those in the bottom 40. One chart in *Shifting Fortunes* shows that the net worth of households in the bottom 40 percent declined by nearly 80 percent between 1983 and 1995. Except for the top 1 percent, the top 40 percent lost ground too—but much less. Today's college teacher, if she is not an adjunct, occupies that relatively lucky top 40 group, while today's clerical worker is in the rapidly sinking bottom 40. Could they still gather comfortably in each other's living rooms to discuss common issues? Do they still have common issues to discuss?

WOMEN GROWING APART

Numbers hardly begin to tell the story. The '80s brought sharp changes in lifestyle and consumption habits between the lower 40 percent—which is roughly what we call the "working class"—and the upper 20 to 30, which is populated by professors, administrators, executives, doctors, lawyers and other "professionals." "Mass markets" became "segmented markets," with different consumer trends signaling differences in status. In 1972, a junior faculty member's living room looked much like that of a departmental secretary—only, in most cases, messier.

Today, the secretary is likely to accessorize her home at Kmart; the professor at Pottery Barn. Three decades ago, we all enjoyed sugary, refined-flour treats at our meetings (not to mention Maxwell House coffee and cigarettes!) Today, the upper-middle class grinds its own beans, insists on whole grain, organic snacks, and vehemently eschews hot dogs and meatloaf. In the '70s, conspicuous, or even just overly enthusiastic, consumption was considered gauche—and not only by leftists and feminists. Today, professors, including quite liberal ones, are likely to have made a deep emotional investment in their houses, their furniture and their pewter ware. It shows how tasteful they are, meaning—when we cut through the garbage about aesthetics—how distinct they are from the "lower" classes.

In the case of women, there is an additional factor compounding the division wrought by class polarization: In the '60s, only about 30 percent of American women worked outside their homes; today, the proportion is reversed, with more than 70 percent of women in the work force. This represents a great advance, since women who earn their own way are of course more able to avoid male domination in their personal lives. But women's influx into the work force also means that fewer and fewer women share the common occupational experience once defined by the word "housewife." I don't want to exaggerate this commonality as it existed in the '60s and '70s; obviously the stay-at-home wife of an executive led a very different life from that of the stay-at-home wife of a blue-collar man. But they did perform similar daily tasks— housecleaning, childcare, shopping, cooking. Today, in contrast, the majority of women fan out every morning to face vastly different work experiences, from manual labor to positions of power. Like men, women are now spread throughout the occupational hierarchy (though not at the very top), where they encounter each other daily as unequals—bosses vs. clerical workers, givers of orders vs. those who are ordered around, etc.

Class was always an issue. Even before polarization set in, some of us lived on the statistical hilltops, others deep in the valleys. But today we are distributed on what looks less like a mountain range and more like a cliff-face. Gender, race and sexual preference still define compelling commonalties, but the sense of a shared condition necessarily weakens as we separate into frequent-flying female executives on the one hand and airport cleaning women on the other. Can feminism or, for that matter, any cross-class social movement, survive as class polarization spreads Americans further and further apart?

UNEQUAL REWARDS

For all the ardent egalitarianism of the early movement, feminism had the unforeseen consequence of heightening the class differences between women. It was educated, middle-class women who most successfully used feminist ideology and solidarity to advance themselves professionally. Feminism has played a role in working-class women's struggles too—for example, in the union organizing drives of university clerical workers—but probably its greatest single economic effect was to open up the formerly male-dominated professions to women. Between the '70s and the '90s, the percentage of female students in business, medical and law schools shot up from less than 10 percent to more than 40 percent.

There have been, however, no comparable gains for young women who cannot afford higher degrees, and most of these women remain in the same low-paid occupations that have been "women's work" for decades. All in all, feminism has had little impact on the status or pay of traditional female occupations like clerical, retail, health care and light assembly line work. While middle-class women gained MBAs, working-class women won the right not to be called "honey"—and not a whole lot more than that.

Secondly, since people tend to marry within their own class, the gains made by women in the professions added to the growing economic gap between the working class and the professional-managerial class. Working-class families gained too, as wives went to work. But, as I argued in *Fear of Falling: The Inner Life of the Middle Class*, the most striking gains have accrued to couples consisting of two well-paid professionals

A Need for Female Unity

Barbara Mehrhof, "On Class Structure Within the Women's Movement."

The ranking of women in a hierarchy achieves significance *only* when women organize among themselves. When women separate off from men in a movement of their own and agitate specifically for "women's rights," the implication is clear that they consider their problems have something to do with the fact that they are women; but whereas in time they may become aware of themselves as a class vis à vis men, they tend to ignore the effects of their distribution in the secondary class structure—that is, what types of males they've been attached to, the ones on the top or the ones on the bottom of the male hierarchy. A situation arises in which all women are glad just to be getting together with other women. The idea emerges that we are all powerless and that the way in which men arrange themselves within their own class has nothing to do with the

or managers. The doctor/lawyer household zoomed well ahead of the truck driver/typist combination.

THE EFFECTS OF CLASS DIVISIONS

So how well has feminism managed to maintain its stance as the ground shifts beneath its feet? Here are some brief observations of the impact of class polarization on a few issues once central to the feminist project:

Welfare. This has to be the most tragic case. In the '70s, feminists hewed to the slogan, "Every woman is just one man away from welfare." This was an exaggeration of course; even then, there were plenty of self-supporting and independently wealthy women. But it was true enough to resonate with the structure women are building among themselves.

In assuming this position, women in the movement are refusing to examine a basic contradiction in our situation: whereas in society *all* women are reduced to a subordinate, minor position in the male/female class system, they are at the same time dispersed among males representing very different levels of power within the male hierarchy. Once women get together on their own without men, this contradiction in their situation will appear for the first time when the women of the upper-class males will move from a minor position in relation to men to a major position in relation to other women. This puts them in a position to oppress other women since the very fact that women are getting together is generating power and the women of the upper classes have been there to grab it so far.

Barbara Mehrhof, "On Class Structure Within the Women's Movement," in Shulamith Firestone (ed.), *Notes from the Second Year*, New York: Radical Feminism, 1970, p. 103–104, 107–108.

large numbers of women who worked outside their homes part time or not at all. We recognized our commonality as homemakers and mothers and we considered this kind of work to be important enough to be paid for—even when there was no husband on the scene. Welfare, in other words, was potentially every woman's concern.

Flash forward to 1996, when Clinton signed the odious Republican welfare reform bill, and you find only the weakest and most tokenistic protests from groups bearing the label "feminist." The core problem, as those of us who were pro-welfare advocates found, was that many middle- and upper-middle class women could no longer see why a woman should be subsidized to raise her children. "Well, I work and raise my kids—why shouldn't they?" was a common response, as if poor women could command wages that would enable them to purchase reliable childcare. As for that other classic feminist slogan—"every mother is a working mother"—no one seems to remember it anymore.

Unhealthy Differences

Health care. Our bodies, after all, are what we have most in common as women, and the women's health movement of the '70s and early '80s probably brought together as diverse a constituency—at least in terms of class—as any other component of feminism. We worked to legalize abortion and to stop the involuntary sterilization of poor women of color, to challenge the sexism of medical care faced by all women consumers and to expand low-income women's access to care.

In many ways, we were successful: Abortion is legal, if not always accessible; the kinds of health information once available only in underground publications like the original *Our Bodies, Ourselves* can now be found in *Mademoiselle*; the medical profession is no longer an all-male bastion of patriarchy. We were not so successful, however, in increasing low-income women's access to health care—in fact, the number of the uninsured is far larger than it used to be, and poor women still get second-class health care when they get any at all. Yet the only women's health issue that seems to generate any kind of broad, cross-class participation today is breast cancer, at least if wearing a pink ribbon counts as "participation."

Even the nature of medical care is increasingly different for women of different classes. While lower-income women worry about paying for abortions or their children's care, many in the upper-middle class are far more concerned with such medical luxuries as high-tech infertility treatments and cosmetic surgery. Young college women get bulimia; less affluent young women are more likely to suffer from toxemia of pregnancy, which is basically a consequence of malnutrition.

Housework. In the '70s, housework was a hot feminist issue and a major theme of consciousness-raising groups. After all, whatever else women did, we did housework; it was the nearly universal female occupation. We debated Pat Mainardi's famous essay on "The Politics of Housework," which focused on the private struggles to get men to pick up their own socks. We argued bitterly about the "wages for housework" movement's proposal that women working at home should be paid by the state. We studied the Cuban legal code, with its intriguing provision that males do their share or face jail time.

A FORGOTTEN ISSUE

Thirty years later, the feminist silence on the issue of housework is nearly absolute. Not, I think, because men are at last doing their share, but because so many women of the upper-middle class now pay other women to do their housework for them. Bring up the subject among affluent feminists today, and you get a guilty silence, followed by defensive patter about how well they pay and treat their cleaning women.

In fact, the $15 an hour commonly earned by freelance maids is not so generous at all, when you consider that it has to cover cleaning equipment, transportation to various cleaning sites throughout the day, as well as any benefits, like health insurance, the cleaning person might choose to purchase for herself. The fast-growing corporate cleaning services like Merry Maids and The Maids International are far worse, offering (at least in the northeastern urban area I looked into) their workers between $5 (yes, that's below the minimum wage) and $7 an hour.

In a particularly bitter irony, many of the women employed by the corporate cleaning services are former welfare recipients bumped off the rolls by the welfare reform bill so feebly resisted by organized feminists. One could conclude, if one was in a very bad mood, that it is not in the interests of affluent feminists to see the wages of working class women improve. As for the prospects of "sisterhood" between affluent women and the women who scrub their toilets—forget about it, even at a "generous" $15 an hour.

The issues that have most successfully weathered class polarization are sexual harassment and male violence against women. These may be the last concerns that potentially unite all women; and they are of course crucial. But there is a danger in letting these issues virtually define feminism, as seems to be the case in some campus women's centers today: Poor and working-class women (and men) face forms of harassment and violence on the job that are not sexual or even clearly gender-related. Being reamed out repeatedly by an obnoxious supervisor of either sex can lead to depression and stress-related disorders. Being forced to work long hours of overtime, or under ergonomically or chemically hazardous conditions, can make a person physically sick. Yet feminism has yet to recognize such routine workplaces experiences as forms of "violence against women."

A RENEWED VISION OF EQUALITY

When posing the question—"can feminism survive class polarization?"—to middle-class feminist acquaintances, I sometimes get the response: "Well, you're right—we have to confront our classism." But the problem is not classism, the problem is class itself: the existence of grave inequalities among women, as well as between women and men.

We should recall that the original radical—and, yes, utopian—feminist vision was of a society without hierarchies of any kind. This of course means equality among the races and the genders, but class is different: There can be no such thing as "equality among the classes." The abolition of hierarchy demands not only racial and gender equality, but the abolition of class. For a start, let's put that outrageous aim back into the long-range feminist agenda and mention it as loudly and often as we can.

In the shorter term, there's plenty to do, and the burden necessarily falls on the more privileged among us: to support working-class women's workplace struggles, to advocate for expanded social services (like childcare and health care) for all women, to push for greater educational access for low-income women and so on and so forth. I'm not telling you anything new here, sisters—you know what to do.

But there's something else, too, in the spirit of another ancient slogan that is usually either forgotten or misinterpreted today: "The personal is the political." Those of us who are fortunate enough to have assets and income beyond our immediate needs need to take a hard look at how we're spending our money. New furniture—and, please, I don't want to hear about how tastefully funky or antique-y it is—or a donation to a homeless shelter? A chic outfit or a check written to an organization fighting sweatshop conditions in the garment industry? A maid or a contribution to a clinic serving low-income women?

I know it sounds scary, but it will be a lot less so if we can make sharing stylish again and excess consumption look as ugly as it actually is. Better yet, give some of your time and your energy too. But if all you can do is write a check, that's fine: Since Congress will never redistribute the wealth (downward, anyway), we may just have to do it ourselves.

CHAPTER 4

FEMINIST FRONTIERS: AMERICAN WOMEN AND THE WORLD

AMERICAN
SOCIAL
MOVEMENTS

War Against Women

GINNY NICARTHY

Ginny NiCarthy, the author of this piece, is a therapist and author whose 1978 book *Getting Free* helped draw public attention to domestic abuse in America. In the present selection, NiCarthy discusses what she sees as a global war against women. According to NiCarthy, in every country around the world women are subject to an epidemic of violence, beating, rape, and murder because they are women. She argues that violence against women is rooted in widespread international acceptance of women's subordination to men, and that if violence against women is to end, women have to speak out, recognize that they are not to blame, and insist that violence is unacceptable. This process began in many countries in the 1970s, NiCarthy says, and she sketches the early stages of international activism against domestic abuse and sexual violence.

'Violence begins early and at home', wrote Canadian Barbara Roberts, quoting figures from the US National Conference on Child Abuse and Neglect in 1981, which showed that one out of four girls in the US is sexually assaulted before she reaches the age of 18, while other studies show one in three. For too many females, violence begins even before birth and ends with femicide—the murder of women. Ultrasound technology and amniocentesis now enable a doctor to identify whether a foetus is male or female, which translates for some prospective parents to 'desirable' (male) or 'expendable' (female). The preference for the male sex over the female is reflected in many ways, from subtle signs and symbols to outright violence throughout life. In India and China, significantly more male foetuses are chosen to live. As many as 99 percent of foetuses aborted in some Bombay clinics were female.

A UNICEF report found that 'a quarter of the 12 million girls born in India annually are dead by the age of 15, many of them victims of neglect, discrimination and sometimes infanticide because of their sex. . . . [A]lthough girls are born biologically stronger, 300,000 more of them die each year than boys. . . .' The World Health Organisation reports that in many countries, girls are fed less, breast-fed for shorter periods of time, taken to doctors less, and die or are physically and mentally maimed by malnutrition at higher rates than boys. Pregnant women and their foetuses suffer malnutrition because of food taboos enforced for pregnant women. Fewer girls than boys go to school, UNICEF says, because 'the tyranny of the household takes over a girl's life as soon as she can perform the simplest task'.

MURDERED WOMEN

At the other end of some women's lives is 'femicide', a word coined in the 1980s to describe murders of women simply because they are women, or because they dare to define for themselves what it means to be a woman. In the past thirty years, the incidence of femicide has grown enormously. In Montreal, Canada, Marc Lepine stormed into an engineering classroom, ordered male students to leave, and turned his semi-automatic rifle on 14 women engineering students, killing them all. He was more explicit than most males who commit femicide, calling the 14 women he murdered 'feminists' and 'viragos'. 'In 1990, in Italy, some 200 women were murdered in circumstances absurdly classified by the mass media as "sexual crimes of passion, of jealousy".' In Washington State, USA, the bones of dozens of young women were found over a period of several years in a wooded area, murdered, police think, by the 'Green River Murderer', a man never found. Most victims of the 'Green River Murderer' were young women prostitutes or women assumed to be prostitutes. Feminists have protested against the sluggish investigation, which they attribute to bias against the presumed lifestyle of the victims. In India,

Bangladesh and Pakistan, in 1987 alone, 8,906 men burned their wives to death, claiming they were suicides or accidents.

A teacher called the dormitory of St. Kizito boarding school in Meru, Kenya, a 'death chamber' after 360 high-school men forced their way in to rape 71 of their fellow students. In the process of their mass assault, 19 women were suffocated or trampled to death as they huddled in fear of the men's attack. It was apparently the killings that called worldwide attention to this event, incidentally exposing the ordinariness of rapes committed by high-school men against women students in Kenyan boarding schools. A woman teacher said, 'The boys didn't mean any harm. They just wanted to rape'. Rape is said to be a common way of boys expressing their frustration when they cannot get what they want.

These headline events are picked almost at random. Every day in virtually every country of the world where men devise and enforce the criminal codes, women are murdered. News of these murders is considered worthy of publication, or not, depending partly on the colour and lifestyle of the victim or perpetrator. When stories are published, the reasons for some of these murders are said to be unknown, so they're dubbed 'senseless'. Others are said to be 'caused' by failure to pay adequate dowry (India), or the 'deranged' state of the killer (Montreal, Washington State) or jealousy (Italy). But the factor that puts each woman most at risk of murder was just that: she was a woman.

SILENCE AND DENIAL

In between foeticide and femicide is an array of horrors perpetrated against women because of their gender. When recorded, estimates are that 40–80 million women are battered by male partners. Many crimes of violence, or legal forms of exploitation and coercion, are directly related to the perpetrator's unwillingness or inability to distinguish between power and sex. Sex demonstrates power; power is sexy. Subordination is 'weakness', even when maintained by law, custom, religion, culture and economics.

Throughout history some women have protested against battering, rape and other violent crimes. Many have gone unrecorded. Among the unsung heroines was twelve-year-old Hauwa Abubakar of Nigeria, who gave up her life rather than live with the man her father married her to four years earlier. Her husband was old enough to be her grandfather. Three times she ran away, and three times she was sent back by her father, who owed the man dowry money. 'Sold' is more accurate than 'married off'. The third time she escaped and was sent back by her father, her husband 'chopped off her legs and genitalia with an axe and Hauwa Abubakar died'.

More often, women have buried the violations under a blanket of shamed forbearance and denial. Some women blame themselves for not speaking out sooner, even when they had little choice. It is true that 'the strongest prisons are built with walls of silence', but there are times when denial of reality—the silence of the mind—enables survival in that prison. No

Many women who sought to gain certain rights and privileges were met with severe opposition and protest.

person can tell another when is the time to deny, and when the time to shout one's outrage from the rooftops. The price of resistance is high. Even to name the crimes can be terrifying.

NAMING THE CRIMES

We have found 'that voice among others like ourselves', that Audré Lorde wrote of, and in twenty years it has grown into an international roar. In 1970 we only whispered the words 'rape' and 'incest'. Whispered, because we had been persuaded that 'those' things only happened to 'other' women, the ones who were strange or bad anyway. Whispered, because most of us had been told the violations were our own fault. Whispered, because the perpetrators warned us not to tell anyone what they did to us, if we wanted to live. We did not even have names for many of the violations against us until the 1970s. We could lament, cry, scream, but we could not articulate our informed rage about them, nor organise against these crimes, while they were, literally, still unspeakable.

Now we have made the crimes speakable. Separately and together, in villages, cities, provinces, states, countries and then, finally, in international forums, we have called them intolerable. In the early 1970s, women began to speak aloud the forbidden words, 'rape' in the US, and 'wife-beating' in Britain, where Erin Pizzey opened the first shelter; in Canada, India, Australia, New Zealand. We said the most dangerous and radical of words: 'It was not my fault'; 'I am not the one to blame'. In the US, the truth gradually emerged that the man who rapes is rarely the monster, the stranger, leaping from the bushes; more commonly it is a man we know, an ordinary, 'sane' man. In England it became apparent that some of the most dangerous men were those who had sworn to love and honour 'until death us do part' and whom women had promised to 'obey'. For the next twenty years women in one country after another would continue to learn, including how death often parts women from their violent husbands. It would be a number of years before we would discover how commonly rape is part of the pattern of battering, and to name it 'marital rape'. It would take still more years for laws in some US and Indian states, and in a few other countries, to recognise marital rape as a crime. In Britain it took until 1991. Additional time would pass before we recognised and named the 'acquaintance rape' and the 'date rape' as pervasive forms of male violation of women.

1975: A Turning Point

In 1975, publications began to proliferate about crimes against women, especially after the United Nations International Women's Year conference in Mexico City. At that conference the official UN Report made only one set of recommendations about violence against women. It suggested steps to improve trials of rapists, and—much more radically, for its time— it recognised marital rape as a crime. The simultaneous NGO conference, 'The Tribune', raised women's consciousness about numerous issues. Grassroots women compared notes on reproductive freedom and the politics of battering and rape. Rape crisis centres had begun to be established during the previous few years in US cities.

In the cities of India women marched, demonstrated and began their own investigations of 'suicides' and 'accidental' deaths of brides in kitchen fires. The payment of dowry had already been outlawed, but feminists continued their protests against its illegal practice. Demands for dowry payments gave an excuse for men to harass—and sometimes murder—their wives. By 1975, Women's Aid, the British coalition of refuges for battered women, brought a more political perspective to woman abuse than the one presented by the shelter's founder. In 1976, the International Tribunal on Crimes against Women took place in Belgium. Women from over 40 countries testified about numerous forms of violence against them. The workshop on violence against women, the largest of the conference, inspired a number of women to establish shelters for battered women in their home countries.

By 1976, we named 'sexual harassment' in the United States, which was later called 'Eve teasing' in India. We said we would no longer accept it as an inevitable part of the environment. We said we wanted it to stop. Like other forms of woman abuse, we could never have predicted the pervasiveness or effects of sexual harassment on women throughout the world. Now we are far more aware. Mexico: 'The Mexican Federation of Women's Trade Unions reports that 95 per cent of women workers are victims of sexual harassment.' USA: 'Forty-two per cent of female (federal) employees . . . reported being sexually harassed at work . . . (during the two years prior to the survey (1981)).' India: '. . . a coalition of women's organisations in Bombay demanded "ladies only carriages" in mass public transit after serious incidents of sexual harassment of women commuting to and from work.' More women in the 12 countries of the European Community complained of sexual harassment than of sex discrimination in their employment.

In 1977, Senegalese writer Awa Thiam noted that interest had begun to surface in stopping excision and infibulation in some African countries. Worldwide, 65-75 million women are victims of some form of genital mutilation. She recognised that these practices were viewed by 'traditionalists' as purification ceremonies and rites of passage. But she insisted on naming them differently: 'Whatever other people may claim,' she said, 'what [the victim] experiences is a "mutilation".' It would be another five years or more before many African governments would take action to discourage or outlaw such practices, or the Inter-African Committee be funded to combat the practices.

INTERNATIONAL CHANGES

In 1978, 128 women from 13 Western countries met in Amsterdam at an international conference on battered women, and agreed that 'women being battered is rooted in an international acceptance of the subordination of women'. In 1977, the Asian Women's Association was formed to defend Korean and Thai women against Japanese sexual exploitation. In 1979, Kathleen Barry described the international traffic in prostitution as the 'sex colonisation' of women. She said, 'forced prostitution and forced marriage, which includes wife battery, veiling, arranged marriages, and polygyny, confirm the subordination of all colonised women'. In 1981, 250 Latin American feminists gathered to exchange ideas at the first Encuentro Latinoamericano y del Caribe, held in Colombia. Two years later, Peru hosted a second conference, where double the expected 300 women participated; they have been succeeded by others, always growing in numbers; the last was held in Argentina.

Throughout the 1970s, international publications on women's issues covered violence against women. Feminist analysis of battering, rape, pornography and incest proliferated in books, films, role plays and pamphlets. Some researchers compared patterns of violence towards women cross-culturally. Knocking down the 'prison-walls' of silence showed us more similarities than we imagined in the victimisation of women in otherwise extremely different cultures. The commonality of our reactions—first shame and denial, then sorrow and sometimes guilt, followed by anger and action—made some of us begin to believe that women live in one 'country'.

In the women's rape crisis centres, health clinics, feminist newspaper offices, law collectives, bookstores and battered women's shelters, women described what men had done to us. We listened to each other. Then we told our stories again, to other women and to the public. We exchanged information about studies reporting how many girls had been forced to have sex with their fathers, step-fathers, uncles, brothers; how many girls were forced into marriage in various parts of the world, forced or driven by poverty into prostitution, or forced to undergo genital mutilation; how many women were battered, killed by husbands, raped; how many murders were claimed to be suicides or accidents. And how many memories of our own humiliation and violation each of us had suppressed. We did not want to admit we were compiling a version of 'body counts', the casualties of war against us. They were not just numbers to us; they were wounded, vibrant, live women. Or dead and mourned sisters.

While we soaked each other's gashes, sat in emergency

rooms, listened and talked, we learned that women needed jobs, lawyers, medical care, child care, money to pay for all these services, group support from peers and a host of other goods and services typically required for people coming out of war zones. Out of our awareness of those needs we began to organise to stop the war against us.

One World Woman's Movement?

In this selection, Chilla Bulbeck, a professor of women's studies and author of numerous books on feminism, class, and culture, discusses the prospects for a united, worldwide women's movement. Bulbeck argues that although women around the world share the condition of being discriminated against because of their gender, the possibility of international feminism is threatened by the legacies of colonialism, slavery, racism, and imperialism, which create great differences among women in different parts of the world. As Bulbeck sees it, there are three possibilities for a worldwide feminism: one, a united movement with men as the enemy; two, a movement that acknowledges the problems of racism and imperialism but insists the chief struggle must be against male domination; or three, a movement that targets many diverse injustices, including those based on gender differences. Bulbeck suggests that this third strategy, with its diverse and multifaceted concerns, may be the best way to approach a global feminist project.

The major problem that women of colour see in joining with western feminists is that they will be asked to break ranks with their male comrades in political struggle, their menfolk, their male workmates. They feel they will be asked to forgo the struggles against racism or imperialism or capitalism and instead be asked to struggle against male violence or state control of women's bodies or husbands' control of the products of women's labour. Being asked to 'forgo' particular struggles in favour of others implies that men do participate in the oppression of women; otherwise a choice would not be required. . . .

One needs to consider whether a global feminism must necessarily put the oppositions starkly, as an 'either' (national liberation) 'or' (feminist struggles) choice. There are perhaps three possible scenarios for describing a global feminism. A global feminist movement might consist of women around the world united under a homogeneous political banner with its enemy being men and patriarchal structures. Or it might be a movement that acknowledges the variations and complexities in the condition of women around the world, accepts the struggles over racism and imperialism but says the major struggle must be the one against male domination. Or it might be a constellation of different localized movements, which movements engage now in a struggle for higher wages for all workers, now in a struggle for freedom from a political regime, now in a struggle for women's control of reproductive choice, and whose members are united by only one belief—that there are forms of oppression based on gender differences and that these must ultimately be addressed if women are to achieve satisfactory autonomy in society. Must the members of any of these suggested movements hate men, be separatists, or can they decide to work with sympathetic men to change their condition?

WOMEN IN SIMILAR SITUATIONS

The potential for a global feminism lies in the apparent similarities of women's position around the world—gender-based mutilation, unequal access to economic, legal and political resources compared with men in each country, and evaluation of women, at least by official culture and most men, as of lesser status, whether by identification with nature, emotion, or some other pollutant of reason or religion. As Elsa Atkin, an immigrant to Australia from Baghdad says: 'It frightens me still that in spite of hundreds of years of different cultural traditions in so many different countries, the issues concerning women are virtually universal and therefore so much harder to change or eradicate.'

The impediments to an international feminism are the differences between women. The results of colonialism, slavery, racism, and imperialism seem to create hierarchies of oppression, hierarchies in which some women benefit from the oppression of others. Ngahuia Te Awekotuku and Marilyn Waring combine the two structures of patriarchy and colonialism to identify fourth world women, women who are an oppressed group within an oppressed group: Maoris, Aborigines, black women in the west, and women in the poor countries, or at least the poorer classes, of the third world. For many fourth world women the oppressions of race and class seem more urgent than the oppressions of gender. They are more immediately preoccupied with economic survival, keeping families together, or national liberation, than they are with violence to women or other gender-based differences within their societies.

DIVERSE GOALS NEED NOT COMPETE

Questions arise then for the possibility of a global feminism. What should be the first priority for women of colour and the third world? Must they consider their interests *qua* women as excluding the possibility of alliances with men? A number of women whose positions were discussed above do not see the interests of women as pre-eminent. By some western definitions this would deny them a definition as feminist. But in the third scenario for global feminism posited above, women do not have to choose to fight only for the specific concerns of women; they may also pursue in addition and sometimes as a priority other objectives they consider more pressing.

The first scenario, that of a homogeneous women's movement, perhaps accords most nearly with the project of international socialism. Marx urged the workers of the world to unite because, he argued, they had more in common with each other in their exploitation through capitalist relations, than they had with national compatriots who were capitalists. However, just as third world women accuse first world women of benefiting from the oppression of their sisters—as consumers of cheaper goods, as beneficiaries of higher wages or better jobs—so did such divisions emerge among the brotherhood of working men. Lenin identified the 'aristocracy of labour', better paid workers in Britain and other imperialist countries, who benefited from the exploitation of cheaper labour in the colonies. In the First World War, working men of the world did not unite but rather enlisted in national armies to kill each other.

Many reasons have been advanced for the failure of international socialism, among them the salience of national identities and the hegemony of conservative or populist ideologies. Others have argued that different living standards and different relations with capital (for example, the so-called 'new middle class') mean that the working class are so internally divided and fractured that they do not recognize the features of their shared exploitation.

THIRD WORLD NATIONALISM

While Virginia Woolf claims (perhaps to some extent in the way that Marx and Engels urged the workers of the world to unite) that nationalism has less appeal to women—'as a woman I have no country'—the struggle of third world women for national liberation shows that many women want a country they can call their own. Similarly, just as there have always been some conservative working men, so are many women deeply conservative. Such women include the marchers of the pots and pans against Allende's regime in Chile, the government-sponsored women's movement in Indonesia, and the revival of Hindu mythological women in India as part of an anti-Muslim and anti-Sikh rhetoric. Conservative women in Sri Lanka claim that women should be wives and mothers, even though Sri Lanka had the first female prime minister in the world, and women have long been able to enter the Buddhist order.

Fanny Tabak points out that in some countries less than 30 per cent of the female population is in the workforce, while those that are employed often do backbreaking low paid work. In such situations, leftwing movements' advocacy of freedom through labour often sounds hollow in comparison with authoritarian regimes' elevation of motherhood. Furthermore, just as first wave feminists were sometimes attacked out of context by postwar feminists as reactionary prudes, so too does the elevation of motherhood make sense—at least as a rhetoric—in societies where husbands desert, or refuse their traditional obligations as a result of the upheavals of 'modernization'. Thus while feminists may argue that conservative women's attempts to make individual husbands support their wives and children are misplaced, they no doubt agree that the position of women in societies where they are dependent on men's support makes this policy attractive. . . .

Those who seek to save the project of feminism argue that women must learn to exploit their differences, to build on them as a basis for political action, not to erase them in the pursuit of a common united front. . . .

VARIED STRUGGLES

The spirit of much of the argument in the foregoing pages commends a catholic [universal] global feminism, the last scenario rather than the first. As such, women as political actors have the freedom to choose their priorities, to choose their battles. However, most feminists would argue that some struggles—for example, the struggle for reproductive freedom or freedom from male violence—require specifically feminist struggles. This is not to say that women united with men in unions have not achieved higher wages for women as well as men, or that national liberation struggles will not improve the position of women in terms of labour force participation and welfare services. It is to say that such struggles must usually run in tandem with other struggles which are specifically feminist if 'sexuality' issues are to be addressed. Women's workforce participation under socialism is not accompanied by extensive childcare facilities or husbands who share the housework; it is premised on the notion that everyone should participate in productive labour. Similarly, and quite naturally, female suffragists could only share platforms with men when they aligned the demand for votes for women with the demand for votes for the working class or votes for negroes. Sometimes they were asked to subordinate the demand for votes for women to the demand for votes for (male) workers or negroes. It is this point, the point when women are asked to choose between a campaign for (some) women and a campaign for (some) men, or a campaign for women which opposes the interests of male comrades (for example, reproductive freedom), that some western feminists would say marks the litmus test of feminist politics. However, to choose on this day, in this struggle, to fight by the side of the men, should not condemn a woman. To fail to see that the choice has been made against some specifically feminist goals, for whatever reason, may perhaps be evidence of ignorance of the feminist project. . . .

If there is only one world, if there are underlying structures of sexual oppression, then a global project should be possible. But this project should not ape the unitary goals of men's political movements. Women, on the whole, can live with more ambivalence and uncertainty than men. Women are trained in the necessity to hear the voices of men, while also experiencing the desire to listen to their own voices. Their subordinate position should make them wary of singular answers, all-pervasive solutions that deny openness to other viewpoints. Thus the world's women's movement need not be 'one', but can be many, modelled on the female symbols of the web or the patchwork quilt. The web and the quilt are made of threads that by themselves are not strong. When stitched together, however, the web and quilt are strong, integrated and eye-pleasing wholes. On the other hand, both the web and quilt are usually created by a single author or to a predetermined pattern. The greatest challenge for all women will be to allow the patchwork to grow, to accommodate one's own work to the shape of other contributions, to allow for the jarring of patterns and colours, but never to lose sight of the project which, as a utopian dream, must be pleasing to the mind's eye, to the eyes of women seeking their strength.

CHAPTER 5

PERSONAL NARRATIVES: VOICES FROM THE VANGUARD

AMERICAN
SOCIAL
MOVEMENTS

An Opening in History

PHYLLIS CHESLER

Phyllis Chesler is a professor of psychology and women's studies and
the author of nine books. In this piece, written as a letter to a young
feminist, Chesler recounts her experience in the women's movement
over the last four decades. For Chesler, the early days of the second
wave of feminism were exciting times during which she and her
feminist colleagues felt young and invincible. At the time, she said,
they didn't yet know how long it would take to achieve their goals,
or about the many personal and political obstacles they would encounter. The heady optimism of the 1960s gave out to long years of
struggle and sacrifice, Chesler recounts, and she and other women
faced discrimination and opposition along the way. Urging young
feminists to recognize that many difficult battles remain, Chesler
concludes by cautioning the younger generation to fight to win
rather than to gain approval from their opponents.

M y generation had it easy. We had no Rolodexes. We
didn't network. We didn't need to. Some of us had been
active in the 1960s civil rights and anti–war movements (I was),
where we had been expected to make the coffee and enable
the men to shine. Some of us came from Ivy League colleges
and suburban marriages, where we had been expected to do
the same damn things. There was a new spirit in the land, a
new organization too: the National Organization for Women.
We joined. We were mainly, but not only, white and educated.
We'd had enough of being handmaids. We were ready to say
goodbye to all that.

One fine day, we opened our front doors and, like [playwright Henrik] Ibsen's Nora, simply walked out. Unlike Nora, we were not alone. There were thousands of women in each city on the move. Overnight, there were thousands of consciousness-raising groups, speak-outs, marches, demonstrations, meetings, campaigns in every major American city, on most college campuses, within many professional associations. It was thrilling, miraculous, unbelievable. The media covered our every statement. Whatever we said was considered news.

We didn't *work* for this; it was ours, an opening in history, a miracle. Overnight, or so it seemed, we formed organizations, ran for public office, sponsored legislation, created rape crisis hotlines and shelters for battered women. Consciousness-raising groups educated and empowered us to enter previously all-male professions. Women became police officers, firefighters, judges, carpenters, lawyers, physicians, electricians, professors, scientists, corporate managers, rabbis, ministers, investment bankers, hard news journalists, editors-in-chief, small business owners. And astronauts. And sports heroes. And armed-forces officers who trained men and flew combat missions themselves.

LIFE WITHOUT FEMINISM

A far cry from the full-time wives, nurses, manicurists, secretaries, shop girls, gossip columnists, actresses, and grade-school teachers of my childhood.

I don't know what kind of life I would have been if there had been no modern feminist movement; a lesser life; a more miserable one, I'm sure. I'll never forget how life gained its fourth dimension, in 1967, when suddenly, the world was bursting with brave, bold, beautiful, adventurous creatures, most of them women. And feminists. It was amazing!

Sure, we Second Wave feminists had more "fun" in the late 1960s. We were young and felt invincible. We had no idea that this struggle would take a lifetime and be much harder than anyone thought. Holding one's own against patriarchy, just holding one's own is not easy. Resisting it—building a resistance movement—would take all we had.

Women's entrance into higher paying jobs did not come easily. Once we became conscious, we still had to fight unimaginably hard for each small gain. But we had each other, which made all the difference. It made having to fight—which we often experienced as "losing"—bearable, possible. Those employers who had refused to hire women in the first place were not happy to do so after we had legally forced their hands. Contrary to most myths about affirmative action, which claim that having quotas lowers standards, most women were in fact over-qualified. Often, a woman has to be twice as good as a man and willing to work twice as hard in a hostile atmosphere in order to keep her job. That is one of the many unwritten job descriptions for women.

CHALLENGES AND OBSTACLES

In the 1970s, I knew women tunnel builders (sandhogs) in New York who were not given sufficient backup or safety information by their male colleagues in the hope that they would fail, even die. I knew women fire fighters, army and navy officers, research physicians, assembly-line workers who were sexually harassed, even assaulted, on the job—then fired if they complained.

Where can a woman file her grievance? After all, Anita Hill was sexually harassed by her boss, Clarence Thomas, who was at that time the head of the Equal Employment Opportunities Commission and is now a sitting Supreme Court justice. I know professional women who were ordered into psychiatric treatment because they alleged sex discrimination. This was—and still is—epidemic; the persistence and courage of the women is nothing less than astounding.

You are entitled to know our war stories. We cannot, in good conscience, send you into battle without giving you a very clear idea of what may happen there.

Great women scientists, such as Barbara McClintock and Rita Levi-Montalcini, who both received Nobel Prizes, only did so when they were already in their seventies and eighties—although they'd been doing extraordinary work for nearly half a century. Marie Curie, the first woman to receive a Nobel Prize, was never admitted to the French Academie des Sciences. Great women must be twice as great and settle for a fraction of the rewards that great men come by sooner and more easily.

At least McClintock and Levi-Montalcini were eventually honored. The scientist Rosalind Franklin died very young of cancer. James Watson, Francis Crick, and Maurice Wilkins (of double helix fame) used Franklin's work without crediting her—work for which *they* received a Nobel Prize. I'd like to propose that Franklin receive posthumous recognition, but what should we do about the ignoble Watson, Crick, and Wilkins, who have enjoyed such honor for so many years?

Given how routinely truly great women have been dishonored, I've been lucky. I had a job and I kept it. I know many supremely accomplished women who were never hired as professors in the first place, whose contracts were not renewed, or who were only allowed to work as adjuncts for tiny sums of money without any security or benefits. I know brilliant, hardworking feminists whom universities undermined, overwhelmed, underpaid, harassed, and fired—long before economic recession/depression set in.

WOMEN IN UNIVERSITIES

What I'm about to describe happened to many radical feminist women lucky enough to have held a university position in the last thirty years.

In 1969–70, I taught one of the first accredited women's studies courses and went on to co-found one of the first women's studies programs in the country. At the time, I was the only woman in my psychology department. Within a year, I had successfully lobbied my all-male colleagues to hire seven (super-qualified) women for ten available positions.

It didn't matter that, overall, women comprised more than 55 percent of the student body and less than 15 percent of the faculty. In my time, the acceptance of even *one* woman into a previously all-male space was enough. Two women? That's a takeover. Seven women? A bloody act of war. I didn't know this, no one warned me—but even if they had, I would have done the same thing, only I'd have been better prepared for battle, less amazed that my actions would provoke unending retaliation. The fact that I was, early on, also associated with the women's class-action lawsuit against our university didn't help. Every principled action I ever took hurt my academic career.

Know that you too may be punished for fighting back, whether you do so alone or with others. But know that if you persevere, you *may* improve the fate of future generations.

I loved teaching, I loved my students. I lectured with passion and devotion. I "hung out" with my students, invited them over for coffee, just as if they were at Oxford or Cambridge, and not at a working-class public institution. Those with power over me sometimes *accused* me of holding extra classes off-campus and verbally threatened me with exposure and expulsion for doing so.

RUMORS AND ACCUSATIONS

By 1972, certain colleagues, administrators, and well-briefed students routinely began to bring charges against me: I was anti-male, I used "sexually explicit" language, I forced my students to read irrelevant feminist works, I didn't "love" my students enough (perhaps the way a Good Mother should). How could I? they reasoned, when I was lecturing, off-campus, on the airwaves, and publishing too!

These charges—and rumors about these charges—had a continuing life of their own during the course of my academic career. Nothing I ever accomplished had as much weight as the rumor that I'd once been accused (never tried, or convicted)—of something, whatever it was.

There we were—beginning to put a strong feminist agenda into place on *their* campuses; there *we* were—founding and attending women's caucuses within the professions, coordinating speak-outs, taking part in televised demonstrations, being quoted in the newspapers, presenting papers at academic conferences, teaching our students differently (better, I think). Each pioneer academic feminist was a local symbol of the national ferment. The patriarchal powers-that-be both feared and hated us, and acted accordingly.

For about ten years, radical feminists were very much in demand on college campuses, on television, in publishing, on legislative panels—but mainly as "dancing dogs." Most pioneer whistle-blowers did not, however, inherit the best academic perches. Those jobs went to ever-younger white men, and then to token numbers of non-radical or anti-feminist women and people of color.

In my case, it took twenty-two years before I was promoted to full professor. Male colleagues with far fewer publications to their credit often accomplished this in ten years. Over the years, those colleagues who kept voting against my promotions actually said, "But you're only publishing things about women! That doesn't count." Or, "You're publishing too much." It took more than twenty-eight years before I was allowed to teach graduate students at my own university.

STILL VULNERABLE

John Demos, in *Entertaining Satan,* a study of the Salem witchcraft trials, points out that people—mainly, but not only, women—were arrested, tried, tortured, and killed as witches not because they *were* witches, but because the Inquisitors were able to get away with it; their victims were vulnerable.

Those accused of witchcraft hadn't really "entertained Satan," nor had the Jews been responsible for Germany's economic tragedy, nor had Moslem and Croatian Bosnians been preparing to destroy the Serbs, nor had the Tutsi in Rwanda been preparing to slaughter the Hutus. False propaganda has always been easily able to arouse barely suppressed hatreds; the rest is tragedy.

After more than thirty years of struggle, I, like many radical feminists, still have very little *institutional* power. Without it, what we know dies with us. Our books do not stay in print long enough to do that work for us; even when they do, they are usually taught only in women's studies classes. Feminist work is not often required reading for everyone. Most of us are not delivering commencement addresses or receiving honorary degrees.

Today, many students—including young feminists—are not familiar with the feminist classics of both the First and Second Waves. Some say that young people today are cynical, not interested in idealistic activism. I disagree—but unless their parents or older siblings were active feminists, they haven't had a chance—at least, not in school, and not in virtual patriarchal reality—to see feminists do these things, over and over again. Like breathing. That's a terrible loss. For me—and for you too.

A Dwindling Presence

Feminist work, even if it's bold and groundbreaking, just has a way of slipping through our collective fingers and down into a living death. I know feminist authors whose work has literally changed the world but who haven't been able to find a publisher for years; I know feminists whose *work* is being taught at the very universities that would never have hired them as professors. Within a decade, we saw some of our greatest feminist ideas distorted, then "disappeared." By the early 1980s, our best consciousness-raising pamphlets and street-corner speeches were forgotten, buried under mounds of reactionary media coverage and sometimes incomprehensible academic papers.

Even as I write, women—people—are dying and here I am, talking about feminist books going out of print! How dare I complain? These feminist visionaries are not dead—although some are; not homeless—although some are; not in jail—although some are. They may be unable to continue their feminist work, but at least they do not have to earn their living on their backs—although some do.

Ultimately, the women at my university won our class-action lawsuit. A judge agreed that the university discriminated against women, but the lawsuit took more than eighteen years, and the remedies were token at best. By the time the lawsuit settled, many of the women in the "class" had died, moved on, retired on shrunken pensions, gotten sick, given up. No one's lost years of productivity and status among their peers were restored.

I am not saying that class-action lawsuits are a waste of time. On the contrary. Recently, however, the federal government has made such suits even harder to bring. (They realize something about the power of collective action.) Without a class-action suit underway, I doubt that many of us could have borne the continued indignities and injustices at work. Without a lawsuit, one by one, we each would have been isolated, humiliated, threatened, fired. Had we tried to speak out as individuals, our allegations might have been brushed off as the misguided beliefs of a few crazy or difficult women. Had we not fought, the next generations of feminist scholars would never have gained even a toehold in the academy.

Fight like hell to transform your educational institutions. But you must also create your own programs, your own schools too. Even if your kitchen-table alternative schools don't last (few do), you'll be full of memories and wisdom, and you will have trained at least a generation or two.

HARASSMENT AND INTIMIDATION

As an academic woman, I was far luckier than women who began working in blue-collar—previously all-male—bastions of power: firefighters, police officers, electricians. As academics, we were (only) verbally intimidated, ostracized, not rewarded for our accomplishments. While some of us were sexually harassed, and re-victimized when we legally "grieved," few of us were physically beaten, firebombed, raped, purposefully exposed to physically dangerous situations by our colleagues as a way of getting us to flee the boys-only club.

The women miners in Eveleth, Minnesota, who worked at the Oglebey Norton company, were not as lucky. Beginning in 1975, these women were subjected to both a physically and sexually hostile work environment. In an ongoing class-action lawsuit, at least nineteen women miners charged repeated incidents of serious and intimidating harassment: a male coworker had ejaculated into a woman's locker; a second male coworker had exposed himself to another woman, then broke into her house and attempted to "embrace her"; a third man had knifed a woman in the leg; a fourth man had simulated choking a woman; a fifth man had physically menaced a woman with a giant dildo; a sixth man threatened to kill a woman whom he called "the little bitch," by "throwing her into the concentrator bins." (Indeed, she would have been ground to bits.) All the women were routinely stalked at home and on the job, referred to as "dogs," subjected to sexual graffiti. Posted outside the personnel director's office was a sign: "Sexual Harassment Will Not Be Reported. However, It Will Be Graded." The union refused to intervene. The women sued.

It took years for the women to establish their right to sue as a class (a precedent decision which has already been used by other women), years before Oglebey Norton was found liable for damages. Then, the Eveleth women were themselves put on trial. Their psychological and gynecological records, including information about past abortions and rapes, were entered into evidence. In the course of this lawsuit, the women have been ostracized by their neighbors. To date, one woman has died, and four women have dropped out. Perhaps the stress of being put on trial was too much to endure.

In 1996, more than twenty years after their ordeal first began, a judge awarded the women miners monetary damages so minimal that they have appealed the decision. [In 1997, an appeals court ordered a new trial to determine fair damages, and the case was settled out of court in 1999.]

You may not be planning to be a miner. You may already be studying to be a lawyer, a stockbroker, a veterinarian, a pilot. Nevertheless, it is important to remember that what happened in Eveleth is what women are still subjected to in America when they try to earn enough money to support themselves and their families.

Submission and humility will not protect you from the injustices of this war. Nothing can. But clarity, and solidarity in action, will allow you to fight back—and to keep sane, no matter what happens.

I was incredibly naive when I was younger. I thought I should be offered a place of honor at the patriarchal table—for my feminist work. I was foolish, but human, for wanting that. It took me time to understand that women—myself included—would remain oppressed for a long time, no matter how fast any individual woman could dance and shine. As Aristotle once wrote: "Revolutions may also arise when persons of great ability, and second to none in their merits, are treated dishonorably by those who themselves enjoy the highest honors."

He was right.

Do not try to win approval from your opponents. Merely fight to win.

While it is important to stand your ground, it is dangerous to get accustomed to standing on it in just one way. I am so used to being opposed that, to this day, I am still surprised, even discomfited, when too many others agree with me. "Have I lost it?" I ask myself, each time. Recently, a young journalist interviewed me. In the midst of my answering his questions, he paused, very sweetly came closer, touched my arm and said, simply, "Phyllis, we're with you. You don't have to make the case from scratch. We're with you."

What Feminism Means to Me

Vivian Gornick

In 1970, when Vivian Gornick was a reporter for the New York newspaper *Village Voice*, her editor sent her to investigate the feminist movement. As Gornick relates in the present essay, within a week she was hooked, and a lifelong involvement with feminism began. For Gornick, feminism offered great solidarity and friendship, and opportunity and encouragement for productive work. Although she avoided and tried to forget about more traditional romantic love, she says, the promise of rewarding romance continued to haunt her, kept at bay only by the companionship she found within the feminist movement. In the early 1980s, as feminism began to lose the solidarity in which Gornick had found comfort, she found herself once again alone, and depression and fear took over. For a while she buried herself in steady work, but eventually she came to see that work, as with romantic love or feminist community, would not be her salvation. Although Gornick acknowledges that her struggles with love and work continue, she says that feminism endowed her with a desire to see things as they are—to see what she calls "hard truth"—and that this endures.

I'd been sent out by the *Village Voice* to investigate "these women's libbers." It was November 1970. "What's that?" I said to my editor. A week later I was a convert.

In the first three days I met Ti-Grace Atkinson, Kate Millett, Shulamith Firestone; in the next three, Phyllis Chesler, Ellen Willis, Alix Kates Shulman. They were all talking at once, and I heard every word each of them spoke. Or, rather, it was that I heard them all saying the same thing because I came away from that week branded by a single thought. It was this: the idea that men by nature take their brains seriously, and women by nature do not, is a belief not a reality; it serves the culture; and from it our entire lives follow. Simple, really. And surely this had already been said. How was it I seemed never to have heard it before? And why was I hearing it now?

It remains one of life's great mysteries—in politics as well as in love—readiness: that moment when the elements are sufficiently fused to galvanize inner change. If you are one who responds to the moment you can never really explain it, you can only describe what it felt like.

I had always known that life was not appetite and acquisition. In my earnest, angry, good-girl way I pursued "meaning." It was important to do work that mattered (that is, work of the mind or spirit), and to love a man who'd be an appropriate partner. These, I knew, were twin requirements: interwoven: one without the other unimaginable. Yet I grew into a compulsive talker who could not bear solitude long enough to study: I did not learn to command steady thought. I read novels, daydreamed an important life, mooned over boys. Although I moralized endlessly about seriousness, it seemed I could pursue the man, not the work. This, however—and here we have something crucial—I didn't know. I did not know I could do love but I couldn't do work. I was always thinking, When things are right I will work. I never thought, How come although things are not right I can still obsess over this boy or that?

In my mid-twenties I fell in love with and married an artist. I was all set. I had a desk to sit at, a partner to encourage me, a sufficiency of time and money. *Now* I would work. Wrong again. Ten years later I was wandering around New York, a divorced "girl" of thirty-five with an aggressive style who had written a couple of articles. Beneath the bluster the confusion was deep, the aimlessness profound. How did I get here? my head throbbed each day, and how do I get out? Questions for which I had no answers until I heard the "women's libbers." It seemed to me then that I saw things clearly. I was old enough, bored enough, exhausted and pained enough. The lifelong inability to take myself seriously as a worker: *this* was the central dilemma of a woman's existence.

JOYFUL MOMENTS

Like Arthur Koestler [a Hungarian born British writer who broke with the Communist Party] getting Marxism for the first time, it was as though light and music were bursting across the top of my skull. The exhilaration I felt once I had the analysis! I woke up with it, danced through the day with it, fell asleep smiling with it. I became impervious: the slings and arrows of daily fortune could not make a dent in me. If I held onto what feminism had made me see I'd soon have myself. Once I had myself I'd have: everything. Life felt good then. I had insight, and I had company. I stood in the middle of my own experience, turning and turning. In every direction I saw a roomful of women, also turning and turning.

That is a moment of joy, when a sufficiently large number of people are galvanized by a social explanation of how their lives have taken shape, and are gathered together in the same place at the same time, speaking the same language, making the same analysis, meeting again and again in New York restaurants, lecture halls, and apartments for the pleasure of elaborating the insight and repeating the analysis. It is the joy of revolutionary politics, and it was ours. To be a feminist in the early seventies—bliss was it in that dawn to be alive. Not an I-love-you in the world could touch it. There was no other place to be, except with each other. We lived then, all of us, inside the loose embrace of feminism. I thought I would spend the rest of my life there.

What went hand in hand with the exhilaration was the quickly formed conviction that work was now something I could not do without. Loving a man, I vowed, would not again be primary. Perhaps, in fact, the two were incompatible. Love-as-I-had-always-known-it was something I might now have to do without. I approached this thought: blithely. As though it would be the easiest thing in the world to accommodate to. After all, I'd always been an uneasy belligerent, one of those women forever complaining that men were afraid of "women like me."

I was no good at flirting, it was a relief to be done with it. If love between equals was impossible—and it looked as though it probably was—who needed it? I pressed myself against my newly hardened heart. The thrill and excitement of feminist reality made me glad to give up sentimentality, take pleasure in tough-mindedness. The only important thing, I told myself, was work. I must teach myself to work. If I worked, I'd have what I needed. I'd be a person in the world. What would it matter then that I was giving up "love"?

MISSING LOVE

As it turned out: it mattered. More than I had ever dreamed it would. Yes, I could no longer live with men on the old terms. Yes, I could settle for nothing less than grown-up affection. Yes, if that meant doing without I was prepared to do without. But the idea of love, if not the reality, was impossible to give up. As the years went on, I saw that romantic love was injected like dye into the nervous system of my emotions, laced through the entire fabric of longing, fantasy, and sentiment. It haunted the psyche, was an ache in the bones; so deeply embedded in the makeup of the spirit it hurt the eyes to look directly into its influence. It would be a cause of pain and conflict for the rest of my life. I love my hardened heart—I have loved it all these years—but the loss of romantic love can still tear at it.

It was always there, threatening, this split in me about love, yet I never spoke of it. I never spoke because I didn't need to speak. I didn't need to speak because it was bearable. It was bearable because I had made an important discovery. The discovery was my secret ingredient, the thing that made my cake rise each morning. It was this: As long as I had a roomful of feminists to come home to I had built-in company for life. I'd never be alone again. The feminists were my sword and my shield: my solace, my comfort, my excitement. If I had the feminists I'd have community, I could live without romantic love. And I was right: I could.

Then the unthinkable happened. Slowly, around 1980, feminist solidarity began to unravel. As the world had failed to change sufficiently to reflect our efforts, that which had separated all women before began to reassert itself now in us. The sense of connection began to erode. More and more, we seemed to have less and less to say to one another. Personalities began to jar, conversations to bore, ideas to repeat themselves. Meetings became tiresome, parties less inviting.

At first, the change in atmosphere among us was only a glimmering suspicion (so solid had feminist comradeship seemed!), but slowly it became an unhappy conviction, and then an undeniable reality. One day I woke up to realize the

Betty Friedan led the campaign to ratify the Equal Rights Amendment and inspired women to become involved in the feminist movement.

excitement, the longing, the expectation of community was: over. Like romantic love, the discrepancy between desire and actuality was too large to overcome.

I fell into a painful depression. Existential loneliness ate at my heart: my beautifully hardened heart. A fear of lifelong solitude took hold of me.

Work, I said to myself. Work hard.

But I can't work hard, I answered myself. I've barely learned how to work steadily, I can't work hard at all.

Try, I replied. And try again. It's all you've got.

The first flash of feminist insight returned to me. Years before, feminism had made me see the value of work; now it was making me see it all over again with new eyes. A second conversion began to take place: the one in which knowledge deepens. I understood that I would have to face alone the very thing my politics had been preparing me for all along. I saw what visionary feminists had seen for two hundred years: that power over one's own life comes only through the steady command of one's own thought.

A sentiment easy enough to declare, the task of a lifetime to achieve.

I sat down at the desk, as though for the first time, to teach myself to stay with my thoughts: to order them, extend them, make them serve me. I failed.

Next day I sat down again. Again, I failed.

Three days later I crawled back to the desk and again I came away defeated. But the day after that the fog cleared out of my head: I solved a simple writing problem, one that had seemed intractable, and a stone rolled off my chest. I breathed easier. The air smelled sweet, the coffee strong, the day inviting.

BREAKING THE LONELINESS

The rhetoric of religious fervor began to evaporate in me, replaced by the reassuring pain of daily effort. I could not keep repeating "work is everything" like a mantra when clearly it *wasn't* everything. But sitting down to it every day became an act of enlightenment. Chekhov's words stared back at me:

"Others made me a slave but I must squeeze the slave out of myself, drop by drop." I had tacked them up over the desk sometime in the early seventies, and my eyes had been glazing across them for more than ten years. Now, I read them again: really read them. It wasn't "work" that would save me, it was the miserable daily effort.

The daily effort became a kind of connection for me. The sense of connection was strengthening. Strength began to make me feel independent. Independence allowed me to think. When I thought, I was less alone. I had myself for company. I had myself, period. I felt the power of renewed wisdom. From the Greeks to Chekhov to Elizabeth Cady Stanton: everyone who had ever cared to investigate the nature of human loneliness had seen that only one's own working mind breaks the solitude of the self.

A hard truth to look directly into. Too hard. And that is why we yearn for love, and for community. Both laudable things to want in a life—but not to yearn for. The yearning is a killer. The yearning makes one sentimental. Sentimentality makes one romanticize. The beauty of feminism, for me, was that it had made me prize hard truth over romance. It was the hard truth I was still after.

Everything I have just written: I have lost sight of times without number. Anxiety, boredom, depression: they overwhelm, they blot me out, I "forget." Slavery of the soul is a kind of amnesia: you cannot hold onto what you know; if you don't hold onto what you know you can't take in your own experience; if you don't take in experience there is no change. Without change the connection within oneself dies. As that is unbearable, life is an endlessness of "remembering" what I already know.

So where does that leave me? In perpetual struggle.

I have endured the loss of three salvation romances—the idea of love, the idea of community, the idea of work. With each loss I have found myself turning back to those first revelatory moments in November 1970. Early feminism remains, for me, the vital flash of clarifying insight. It redeems me from self-pity, bestows on me the incomparable gift of wanting to see things as they are.

I still struggle with love: I struggle to love both my hard heart, and another human being at the same time—and with work: the daily effort remains excruciating. But when I make the effort I am resisting the romance. When I resist the romance—look steadily at as much hard truth as I can take in—I have more of myself, and feminism lives in me.

Confessions of a Former Man Hater

KAY LEIGH HAGAN

Kay Leigh Hagan leads writing and feminist study groups and is the author of several books. In this article, she talks about how her attitudes toward men have changed. During her first few years as a feminist, she says, she was busy rethinking and challenging adopted customs and ideas, and this led her to alter her view of men. Hagan noticed, she says, the injustice of sexism everywhere around her and she viewed all men as responsible for it and as benefiting from it. Only later, she recounts, when a colleague suggested she think about racism, classism, and ableism, did she realize that as a white, middle-class, able-bodied person, she too had benefited from injustices. This realization, she believes, made it possible for her to empathize with men, and she no longer thinks hating men is the best way to confront sexism in the world. The problems of sexism, racism, and classism are very deep, she thinks, and call for alliances among men and women.

I remember well my first conscious exchange with a Good Man. Tom was the best friend of a man I had been dating for several months, and a warm acquaintance—though hardly a friend—of mine. I had asked him to meet me for coffee one day after a troubling incident with my lover when I feared he might hit me. He had not, but as I closed and locked the door behind him that night, I was shaken by the possibility. And I was also deeply in love. I called Tom for a "reality check," to find out if he knew of any history of physical violence, and to seek his advice.

After listening carefully to my fitful story, he asked, "How much abuse do you think you ought to tolerate in this relationship?" I only had to consider this for a moment. "Well, some. I mean, if I'm serious about him, and if I want the relationship to work, to last, there will be ups and downs. I don't think I should run away when it gets hard. I should be willing to tolerate a little abuse if I really love him." Tom paused, looked me gently but directly in the eyes, and said, "Kay, in a loving relationship, abuse is unacceptable. You should not have to tolerate any abuse to be loved." This surprising notion had not entered my mind.

Something in my worldview, in my self-esteem, in my understanding of love and power changed forever in that moment. What had I expected from Tom? Certainly that he would defend his friend, reassure me that he would never be violent, tell me everything would be okay, perhaps volunteer to talk to my lover. Instead, his reaction encouraged me to love myself, to take responsibility for my own well-being, and to reject violence even in its subtler forms. I did not expect him to hold up a compassionate mirror to the historical legacy of sexism I was playing out unwittingly in my own partnership. I did not expect Tom to be my ally—this was another option I had not considered.

What enabled him to respond in this way? As it happens, Tom later became one of the founders of an organization dedicated to stopping male violence against women. His insight was based, I know now, on years of study and self-reflection using a feminist analysis of power to understand the context and range of men's abusive behavior toward women, starting with his own. This first experience with a man who has taken both a personal and public stand against male supremacy was not my last, but its intimate nature left an indelible impression on me. I sensed the revolutionary potential of radical alliances between men and women, and I decided to believe in them. I am proud to say that I have several such male allies in my life today. The lover referenced above is not among them.

What should women expect from our male allies—our partners, relatives, lovers, friends, neighbors, coworkers, colleagues— those men we love and respect, who claim to love and respect us? Some of the answers to this question may lie in its opposite.

I spent my first years as a feminist discovering the world anew: suddenly I realized society as I had accepted it was not necessarily the only way society could be. Applying this new political template to my observations, it appeared for the most part that society was in fact constructed by those in power for their benefit at the expense of others—most emphatically (I noted at the time), by men at the expense of women. Further, I was disturbed to discover that by my lack of consciousness, I cooperated with this situation, even colluding with my own oppression in many ways. Already an aficionado of the examined life, I became quite fascinated with the dilemma of internalized oppression. In truth, I was mesmerized by it.

For some years, identifying all the ways women are oppressed consumed me in a righteous fury. Having not understood for my first thirty years that male supremacy is a ruse, I made up for lost time by reading, writing, and reconsidering my assumptions and perceptions about men and women. I began to move through the world in a different way, nurturing myself, questioning authority, replacing men with women in the center of my life, and generally affirming women in any way I could, most importantly at this point in my own choices.

Understandably, in that early rush of liberation I found myself relating to men differently, often confronting them about assumptions of privilege and superiority. After years of accepting sexism as "just life," suddenly I noticed its injustice everywhere, and viewed all men as its perpetrators and benefactors. I felt disgusted with the basic attitudes of men in general: how disturbed they were when I spoke up, how defensive and offended they acted when faced with their history of unjust advantage, how conveniently ignorant they professed to be of their artificially heightened status. Having shifted from the extreme of obedient denial to its opposite of hypervigilance, I found men, as a whole, insufferable. I recall it was during this period that I was first accused of being a man-hater. Although I intuited the fallacy of this charge at the time, I could not verbalize a defense because, on some visceral level, the label felt accurate. However, I was to learn over the years that even a woman's slightest deviation from utter devotion to male supremacy is likely to be deemed "man-hating," or at the very least "male-bashing." The visceral resonance I felt was actually the thrill of breaking that taboo.

THE TURN

Of course, as my initial focus of scrutiny I would be compelled by that area where I felt most comfortable: as a target of oppression. But feminism, honestly pursued, does not allow its advocates to settle in to such a position for long. More than any other discipline, philosophy, spiritual path, belief system, or worldview I've encountered, feminism requires that we keep asking questions, that we make connections, especially those that disturb our assumptions. When a wise activist colleague suggested—more than once—that I might consider widening my area of inquiry and self-observation to include other forms of oppression, such as racism, classism, and ableism, I eventually took her advice. And promptly stumbled over the dead elephant in the living room.

In these social constructions, my position was not nearly so enchanting to me. With white skin in a white supremacist system, middle-class status in a classist system, full mobility, vision, and hearing in a system that despises disability, I was flipped to the other side of the injustice equation. The dead elephant in the living room of my self-esteem was privilege: that inheritance of profound institutionalized advantage I possessed—unbidden, unearned, and previously invisible to me—bestowed by a system that arbitrarily prized and rewarded certain of my characteristics. Particularly confusing was the fact that I seemed to believe I deserved these advantages, on the basis of—what? My whiteness? My mobility? My college degree? This was, after all, the same system I railed against for its absurd gender hierarchy. Did I believe that receiving advantages from such a system was valid and moral, that only its dispensation of penalty and restriction was objectionable? Clearly my socialization, which I was carefully examining for evidence of internalized messages of inferiority, also included an intricate set of expectations based on presumptions of superiority. It occurred to me that if I stand against oppression, then I must stand against privilege as well. Mustering a reluctant determination, I now became obsessed with understanding my internalized privilege with the same depth as I was learning to understand my internalized oppression. Onward through the fog.

THE PERILS OF PRIVILEGE

While I am at the early stages of what clearly will be a lifelong pursuit, at the outset I can tell it is not going to be easy. Privilege is quite smarmy, marked by a kind of arrogant ignorance. (Prince Charles comes to mind here.) Where oppression casts us into the sharp-edged realms of deprivation and desperation without a buffer, privilege creates a cushion of distance and protection from the "great unwashed," fostering a distorted sense of reality framed by willful ignorance. Becoming more aware of privilege does not exactly fill me with that warm glow I experienced earlier in relation to my rekindled female pride. Indeed, for people of conscience, acknowledging privilege is not nearly as fun as claiming oppression. Rage and righteousness are much more appealing to me than regret and reparations. The connections feel harder to make, and my resistance is difficult to overcome, indeed, even to perceive as such. Nevertheless, certain benefits of this inquiry are already becoming obvious. As I work to raise my consciousness and to discern how to be an ally to people of color, poor people, and people with disabilities despite my privilege in these areas, I have had an epiphany concerning men. Where once I was mystified by what seems to be their complete denial of a social system that systematically advantages them for being male, I realize now they are simply wrapped in the soft prison of their privilege—as I am. Suddenly, I can empathize.

THE BIG PICTURE

> The conundrum humanity faces is this: We are on a sinking ship, but the only materials we have to build a ship that

will float come from the ship itself. The problem is that: we must tear down the old ship before it sinks, rebuilding it at the same time without destroying the needed parts.

—Joel Kramer and Diana Alstad, *The Guru Papers*

My most optimistic read of contemporary society is that we are in a long and awkward transition phase from Patriarchal Hell to Feminist Utopia. In short, this Hell valorizes authoritarianism—expressed by the practices of supremacy and submission—and in it we have each inherited a mixture of unearned privilege and undeserved oppression. Feminism, often myopically caricatured as a "battle of the sexes," is in fact a social change movement challenging the very concept of domination as an ethical organizing principle. By questioning male supremacy and the gender caste structure that implements it, feminism reveals the seminal elements of the system of dominance as a whole, exposing the connections and shared values among sexism, racism, heterosexism, classism, and other oppressive social structures. The worldwide historical resistance to challenging sexism might indicate its position in domination's house of cards.

While I am consistently rewarded for being white, educated, able-bodied, and middle-aged, I am penalized for being female and lesbian. Most of us experience such a mixture of superiority and subordination, and move mindlessly through the culture, responding automatically to the overt and covert cues prompting behaviors and beliefs appropriate to our relative social status in the immediate situation. While we frequently perceive neither our oppression nor our privilege, we maintain and collude with both by our daily choices—a state of being Mary Daly has called Robotitude. The mission of people of conscience, as I view it, is to become conscious of this value system and how it affects us, to reclaim our right to self-determination, then to shift the paradigm however we can, at whatever level possible, to the said Feminist Utopia, a place where all have enough, kindreds make communities, mutual respect and compassionate conflict reign, the earth is sacred, universal safety is the rule, and domination, oppression, and privilege are nonsense terms. Riane Eisler speaks of the shift from a culture of dominance to a culture of partnership. While it may seem a long way from here to there, the first essential steps—being internal ones—are always at hand.

I believe the role of feminist advocates here is that of a "transition team" for this paradigm shift. Like the transition teams that facilitate the peaceful shift of power from one presidential administration to another, feminist advocates are uniquely qualified to stimulate society's shift from dominance to partnership. Feminism provides an analysis of power that demystifies the compelling culture of domination, as well as a societal vision that defines an appropriate strategy for change. As we strive to comprehend the ways all of us have been indoctrinated into Patriarchal Hell (a social order, by the way, that has had over five thousand years to establish itself), we must work together to actualize in practical and daily ways the shift from one value system to another, to create bridges of transition to a culture of partnership, to be living heralds of that utopian world. We cannot know how long this task will take, but the task itself is upon us: our ship is sinking, and we need all the help we can get. I bring all this up to emphasize the critical importance of allies. In spite of our individual inheritance of privilege and oppression, we must find ways to build alliances with those who share our values and vision. Subscribing to this larger view of feminism has prompted another important change in my personal stance: from "man-hater" to recruiter.

RADICAL ALLIANCES

The identification of potential allies in this quagmire is definitely a challenge. While oppression binds us in a straitjacket of deprivation and self-loathing, privilege numbs us in a medicated haze of denial and self-aggrandizement. Whatever our particular mix of privilege and oppression, we move into awareness and self-determination accompanied to some degree by outrage, shame, despair, guilt, resentment, cynicism, defensiveness, and suspicion. Trust, a necessary aspect for alliance, seems unlikely. Even foolish. How to do this?

After taking some tentative steps to challenge the skewed internal perspectives created by both oppression and privilege, I am coming to understand that I can learn something about how to be an ally by drawing from my lived experiences in each to inform the other. To wit: when men or heterosexuals seem insensitive and arrogant to me, I can mentally change places—visit my race privilege, for instance—to get an intimate clue about their exasperating attitudes. Well-intentioned offenders may need only a gentle reminder to adjust their sensibilities, while the ingrained supremacist requires a more assertive intervention or a wider berth. And when I feel confounded, defensive, or hurt by the anger of people of color or people with disabilities toward me or the system in general, I can visit my experience of oppression as a woman and lesbian to gain some insight into their urgency and impatience with my inability—or unwillingness—to "get it." I can remember how vitally important it is to be believed, even if I am not understood. By using this internal shift of perspective, I can sometimes circumvent the kneejerk reactions of resignation and retreat that prevent me from taking action, speaking up, reaching out, or otherwise creating the opportunity for change, for connection, for alliance.

In grappling with the dilemma of privilege, I have often wished those who are victimized by it would just, please, tell me what to do to make it right, to fix it, to get it. While I understand the inappropriateness of asking the targets of oppression to educate the perpetrators, I have found also that the protected condition of privilege itself can inhibit me from becoming aware of the very characteristics I must change in order to become trustworthy and authentic—that is, to become a potential ally myself. The privilege of privilege is not having to acknowledge my privilege. Oddly, a stock Christian image seems helpful here: Christ—or in this case, perhaps, Nemesis—is knocking at the door, but there is no latch on the outside. The door can be opened only from within. I believe the soft prison of privilege has such a door. While I have honed with zeal the ability to detect the many ways I collude with my own oppression, I have a great deal of difficulty—or probably more accurately, resistance to—identifying the more subtle, daily practices of my privilege, both internalized and bestowed. Only to the extent that I can do this am I able to challenge those practices and make the choice to use my privilege with integrity. This is the message of Nemesis.

LOOKING FOR MR. GOOD

> The road men are taking toward the goal of liberation has but one obstacle that will prevent them from reaching the mark of transforming growth we call liberation; that obstacle is male supremacy.
>
> —Harriet Gill, "Men's Predicament: Male Supremacy"

So how can women recognize our potential allies among men? The likely candidates—the Good Men—do exhibit distinguishing characteristics. Here are some that come to mind:

Men who are allies of women acknowledge and reject the notion of male supremacy and the unjust gender caste system that supports it. They understand that while they are not personally responsible for creating this system, they have inherited its benefits and internalized its values. Because they take a stand against this belief—in public and in private—they are often regarded by most other men as defectors from patriarchy. Good Men cop to male privilege; they wrestle with it, work on it, worry about it, and always strive to use it with integrity.

For both men and women, Good Men can be somewhat disturbing to be around because they usually do not act in ways associated with typical men: they listen more than they talk; they self-reflect on their behavior and motives; they actively educate themselves about women's reality by seeking out women's culture and listening to women while not imposing themselves on sacred ground. They avoid using women for vicarious emotional expression; they can offer observations about a woman's internalized oppression without judgment or sarcasm; they ask permission before touching. When they err—and they do err—they look to women for guidance, and receive criticism with gratitude. They practice enduring uncertainty while waiting for a new way of being to reveal previously unconsidered alternatives to controlling and abusive behavior. They intervene in other men's misogynist behavior, even when women are not present, and they work hard to recognize and challenge their own. Perhaps most amazingly, Good Men perceive the value of a feminist practice for themselves, and they advocate it not because it's politically correct, or because they want women to like them, or even because they want women to have equality, but because they understand that male privilege prevents them not only from becoming whole, authentic human beings but also from knowing the truth about the world. They continue to open the door.

Because they offer proof that men can change, the Good Men in my life have ruined me forever as a man-hater—I am unable to believe that men, as a lot, cannot be redeemed. Granted, I have lapsed into this view before, and no doubt will do it again when the next unthinkable incident of male violence against women crosses my path. There are times when man-hating seems the appropriate response. But ultimately, I believe that man-hating is the easy way out: not only does it oversimplify a deep and complex problem (and thus prevent us from finding any real solutions), but in a strange way it lets men off the hook. The demonized man can easily be dismissed as hopeless. But when I dare to expect more of men, to insist on their full humanity, intelligence, and responsibility, the image of an ally emerges and working together becomes a possibility.

Radical allies across privilege and oppression give a most precious gift when we tell the truth about ourselves and what we perceive about each other. Which is to say, once again, what may appear to some as man-hating may very well be something else far less personal, something broader with more historical context, something about changing the world.

Gender Blender

JENNIFER REID MAXCY MYHRE

Jennifer Reid Maxcy Myhre is used to people not knowing whether she is a man or a woman, and she doesn't mind. One day, she says, she got tired of having to spend so long in front of the mirror making her hair presentable, so she got a crew cut, traditionally a men's haircut. A lot of people don't like her appearance, which includes unshaven armpits and legs, Maxcy Myhre says. As she sees it, though, her appearance is natural, and people who dress in specifically men's outfits or specifically women's outfits are fitting into a system in which people are judged based on their gender. Maxcy Myhre hopes that "gender blenders," as she calls herself, will help interrupt that system and challenge accepted ideas about men and women. She believes that femininity is a socially constructed concept that is linked to the oppression of women, and so, for her, an important part of feminism is not being feminine.

"Daddy, is that a boy or a girl?" I hear the six-year-old girl whisper the question to her father as I pass by. I smile at her; she articulates aloud what the adults around her are thinking. Her question does not offend me in the way that the "What are you, some kinda monk?" from the burly man in the fast-food restaurant, or the "Hey, is that a fag?" shouted at me from behind as I walk hand in hand with a man down the street, offends me.

I have a crew cut. I also don't shave my leg or armpit hair, but these are surprisingly unimportant details compared to my near-baldness. I have a look that some people call androgynous and others call butch. Daily I face stares, questions and rude comments, and harassment by those who believe that they have the right to pass judgment on my appearance and thus on my person. I am often amazed by the audacity of complete strangers who think it is perfectly acceptable to come up and touch my head. Occasionally, I get looks of envy and plaintive whispered comments from women in elevators: "I wish I had the courage to do that."

When I first began to think about shaving my head, it really wasn't a political statement, or so I thought at the time. I got tired of the blow-drying and curling and hair spraying I had to do to make my hair look presentable. So finally I decided to do it. I was in college and nobody cared what I looked like. I called a salon and asked for someone who would be willing to use the clippers.

When I arrived at the salon (you know, the kind that charges a certain amount to cut men's hair and then charges more if you're a woman, because your hair is inherently more difficult and intractable), I was seated and asked to wait. I was informed that Fifi would be cutting my hair this afternoon. When Fifi wiggled over to me, wearing little slinky gold shorts and tottering on gold high heels, I saw that she had a voluminous mane of hair. I became a bit worried. I tried to make it clear that I wanted my hair cut short, a crew cut. Forty-five minutes later, she still hadn't gotten the clippers out and was exclaiming that she could make me look just like Brigitte Nielsen. No thanks. Had it been now, I would have gotten uppity and insisted on the clippers, but both being assertive and shaving my head was a bit much to ask at the time. In my dorm laundry room, a friend and a pair of clippers finally got the job done.

A Renewed Feminism

I got my crew cut about a year and a half after what I call my feminist rebirth. Even as a child, I considered myself a feminist, supported the ERA [Equal Rights Amendment] (even though I knew very little about it) and was quick to react to statements from junior high classmates that women should be barefoot and pregnant. I had a mother who was employed and a father who was as involved as my mother in raising me. In eighth grade, I wrote a paper on the history of the women's suffrage movement in the U.S. In ninth grade, I read *Against Our Will*. But for all this, when I look back now I feel that politically I've traveled light-years from where I was then.

My feminist rebirth came during my college years. One summer, I stuffed the ideas of Millett, Brownmiller and Walker into my eager head. Some of us come to feminism because of abuse, harassment, eating disorders. I came to feminism because I hated shaving my legs. That summer I started to appreciate the amount of time, labor and money women put into their appearance in order to become "women," which in our culture is synonymous with "not-men."

Femininity isn't inherent, natural or biological. It takes work to look like a "woman," and this is evident when one looks at female impersonators and drag queens—men, with the same work, can look just like "women." Put on a pair of high heels and some lipstick and you're halfway there. The disguise is amazingly effective; most people are fooled by good female impersonators. The hullabaloo over the movie *The Crying Game* is testimony to the power of the trappings of femininity—long hair, makeup, dresses, high heels—in shaping our judgments of gender.

So to christen my feminist rebirth, I quit shaving my legs. I threw away my high heels and my tight skirts, my makeup and my jewelry. I grew out my armpit hair, and I talked like a woman with a mission. Why should I have to waste all that time and effort when I looked perfectly fine as I was? Giving up my "femininity" was my first action as a feminist. I didn't consider myself any less of a woman, but not working at looking like a woman meant that most people considered me masculine. I chose to call myself androgynous and hoped to destroy the distinction between masculine and feminine, male and female.

No Slave to Appearance

I became a feminist activist after that summer and helped to found a campus organization called Supportive Students Against Sexual Assault. As I became more engaged in working to stop violence against women, my outrage at women's slavery to their appearance subsided somewhat. It became a side issue, a conversation piece. That's about the time when I shaved my head, not really considering it a political statement, only knowing that I had burned my hand on my curling iron once too often. Now I consider it one of the most profound, daily statements of my feminist struggle. I spend less than one minute on my appearance each day, which saves me valuable time that I can choose to fill as I please—keeping myself sane, changing the world. The way I look is a constant slap in the face to those who believe that the boundaries between masculine and feminine are clear and rigid, inherent and right.

My appearance rarely escapes notice. I make people feel extremely uncomfortable. I have been called "butch," I have been called "dyke" and I have been mistaken for a man more times than I can remember. I have been told to wear big earrings and bright red lipstick so that "people can tell." I have been told that someday I will fall in love with a man who will change my mind about shaving my legs. (I can see it now—the romance novel: Rolf, with his commanding presence and masculine charm, shows me the error of my feminist and unfeminine ways. He and I get married; I give up my career and devote myself happily to raising our children. Harlequin would love that plot.)

While these comments often offend me, I find them telling, illustrative of the attitudes people hold about appearance, femininity and masculinity. People are uncomfortable around me because I do not, at first glance, fit easily into a gender category. This is very alarming to homophobic people; after all, if people aren't easily distinguishable as male or female, we run the risk of becoming attracted to a person of the same sex. Homophobic people avoid this risk by avoiding gender blenders like myself. Many people react to me with confused glances and embarrassed stammers; often they avoid eye contact. I am glad they are uncomfortable; it suits my purposes.

Regardless of their possession of X or Y chromosomes, we base judgments of gender on people's appearance—their secondary sex characteristics, their demeanor, their style of dress, their hair. We all hold in our minds a blueprint of our perceptions of femininity and masculinity. In a nutshell, femininity consists of having longish hair; wearing makeup, skirts, jewelry and high heels; walking with a wiggle; having little or no observable body hair; and being in general soft, rounded (but not too rounded) and sweet smelling. This nutshell is important because a woman's attractiveness to men is the primary measure of her worth. How often have you heard women actors on talk shows (or any woman, for that matter, in almost any situation) introduced with an adjective about their beauty rather than their talent? How often have you heard both men and women pass judgment on an ugly woman's merits as a person? How often have you heard comments about women sleeping their way to the top, as if sexual attractiveness were the only quality that could earn them such status? A woman's value is gauged according to her appearance, and women are expected to comply with standards set by society.

What is our reward for this constant attention to detail, our ever-vigilant concern with our appearance? The acceptance and approval of those (often men, occasionally women) in power. Those who break too many of the stereotypes are made to pay with social disapproval. A woman can wear her hair short, but not too short. She can forgo makeup as long as she wears earrings. If she doesn't follow the rules, she will be labeled unfeminine, manlike, butch. These are words that provoke an immediate recoil. These are words that antifeminists have used to keep women silent; they are words we must learn not to be afraid of.

Unpopular but Unrepentant

I am one of those feminists that are made so much of in the media: a hairy-legged, strident, "masculine" woman, a "manhater" (another word for women who choose to tell the truth about men and patriarchy). I am a feminist with whom even other feminists are sometimes uncomfortable: "She gives the rest of us a bad name."

Rather than shrinking from words like "masculine" and "butch," we should point out why we are called these names and how male supremacy is served if we keep silent in fear of being called these names. We are called masculine when we act as we please, when we take control of our bodies and lives, when we speak out loud and refuse to be silenced, when we assert the dignity of our persons and our right to self-determination, when we are ambitious, courageous, sexy and proud. We are called butch when we decide that an hour in front of the mirror or the closet is better spent helping women, making money, learning, having sex, laughing with friends or raising children. We are called butch when we decide that those eight hours on high heels hobble us and prevent us from fighting back. We are called butch when we become indifferent to the male gaze. We are called masculine and butch in order to keep us in our place, to scare us, to gag and silence us.

So I don't flinch anymore when I am addressed as "Sir." I don't flinch at the pointed fingers and whispers, at the outright harassment. I hold my head up (and swagger, occasionally, when I get carried away). I refuse to live my life in a box labeled "Female." In my more ambitious and perhaps foolishly hopeful moments, I imagine a world in which there is no simple categorization by sex, no gender, but only people. I imagine a world in which I am no longer stared at. I imagine a world in which people are attracted to me not because of what sex I am (or appear to be) but rather because they find me fascinating. I imagine a world in which I am at home.

CHRONOLOGY

1776

Abigail Adams asks her husband, John, to "remember the ladies" as he writes the new laws during the second Continental Congress.

1826

The first public high schools for girls open in New York and Boston.

1827

Isabella Bonfree is freed from slavery. She later takes the name Sojourner Truth and becomes a leading activist for the rights of women and black people.

1829

Frances Wright travels across the country on a paid lecture tour, criticizing organized religion for giving women a secondary role and advocating easier access to divorce and birth control.

1833

Oberlin College in Ohio becomes the first co-education college in the country.

1837

Mary Lyon founds Mount Holyoke College in Massachusetts, which later becomes the first four-year college for women in the country.

1838

Angelina Grimke becomes the first woman in the United States allowed to address a legislative body. She speaks in Massachusetts for two hours on the cruelty of racism.

1840

Elizabeth Cady Stanton and Lucretia Mott meet at an anti-slavery convention in London. They are denied the chance to give speeches or vote because they are women, which motivates them to begin advocating women's rights.

1841

Oberlin College graduates its first class: Mary Hosford, Elizabeth Smith Prall, and Caroline Mary Rudd.

1848

The first women's rights convention in the United States is held in Seneca Falls, New York. The Declaration of Sentiments and Resolutions is passed. Maria Mitchell, an astronomer, becomes the first woman elected to the American Academy of Arts and Sciences. Nearly one hundred years pass before a second woman is added.

1849

Lily, the first prominent women's rights newspaper, is published by Amelia Jenks Bloomer.

1850

The Female Women's Medical College of Pennsylvania is opened by Quaker doctors to give women a chance to study medicine. When the first women graduate, they do so under police guard because of threats of violence.

1855

Lucy Stone gets married and keeps her own name, the first woman on record to do so.

1861

Vassar College in Poughkeepsie, New York, a women's college, opens.

1862

Mary Jane Patterson receives a full baccalaureate degree, the first African American woman to do so, from Oberlin College.

1866

Elizabeth Cady Stanton and Susan B. Anthony found the American Equal Rights Association, which fights for universal suffrage.

1868

The Fourteenth Amendment is ratified, which gives all citizens equal protection under the law.

1869

The women's movement splits into two groups over the issue of whether to support the Fifteenth Amendment which would give the vote to black men. Lucy Stone, Henry Blackwell, and Julia Ward Howe organize the American Woman Suffrage Association in Boston, which supports the amendment. Elizabeth Cady Stanton and Susan B. Anthony form the New York–based National Woman Suffrage Association, which wants the amendment scrapped in favor of one that gives the vote to black men and to white and black women.

1870

The Fifteenth Amendment is passed.

1872

Susan B. Anthony is arrested and tried in Rochester, New York, for trying to vote in the presidential election. Sojourner Truth appears at a polling booth in Michigan demanding a ballot but is turned away.

1873

The Supreme Court rules in *Bradwell v. Illinois* that a state can bar a married woman from practicing law. One judge writes "the natural and proper timidity and delicacy which belongs to the female sex evidently unfits it for many of the occupations of civil life."

1875

In *Minor v. Happersett,* the Supreme Court rules that women are persons, but adds that women are a "special category of non-voting citizens." Michigan and Minnesota give women the right to vote in school board elections. Smith College in Northhampton, MA opens, the first women's college founded and endowed by a woman. Wellesley College, another women's college, just outside of Boston opens.

1877

Helen Magill earns a doctorate in Greek from Boston University, the first woman to receive a Ph.D. in the United States.

1878

An amendment to give the vote to women is introduced in Congress, but fails.

1890

The two major national women's rights organizations are united as the National American Woman Suffrage Association, headed by Elizabeth Cady Stanton.

1894

Colorado adopts a state amendment giving women the right to vote.

1902

Elizabeth Cady Stanton dies.

1905

Former President Grover Cleveland writes, "Sensible and responsible women do not want to vote."

1906

Susan B. Anthony dies. In her last public speech she says "Failure is impossible."

1913

The Congressional Union, later known as the National Women's Party, is founded by Alice Paul and Lucy Burns. Members picket the White House and go on hunger strikes to gain publicity for women's suffrage.

1914

The National Federation of Women's Clubs, with over two million female members, endorses women's suffrage. *Women Rebel*, published by Margaret Sanger, calls for legal contraception. The Post Office bans it.

1916

Jeannette Rankin of Montana is elected to the U.S. House of Representatives, the first woman so elected. The first birth control clinic in the United States is opened in Brooklyn, New York, by Margaret Sanger and her sister Ethel Byrne. Ten days later it is shut down and the women are arrested, tried, and imprisoned.

1917

The National Women's Party pickets the White House, starting in January, and remains there despite freezing temperatures and harsh public response. In October, 168 members are arrested and convicted for picketing. In prison they stage hunger strikes but are force-fed. They are eventually released.

1918

Woodrow Wilson changes his stance on suffrage, and delivers a speech to the Senate encouraging legislators to support an amendment giving women the vote.

1919

The Nineteenth Amendment, written over forty years earlier by Susan B. Anthony, is passed by both houses of Congress and heads to the states for ratification. The House of Representatives votes 304 to 89; the Senate votes with just two votes to spare, 56 to 25.

1920

The Nineteenth Amendment is ratified August 26.

1921

The American Association of University Women is formed. Margaret Sanger founds the American Birth Control League, which becomes the Federation of Planned Parenthood in 1942.

1923

The National Woman's Party proposes the Equal Rights Amendment to bar sex discrimination.

1953

Simon De Beauvoir's book, *The Second Sex*, is published in the United States.

1960

The birth control pill is approved.

1961

John F. Kennedy appoints the President's Commission on the Status of Women, which is headed by Eleanor Roosevelt.

1963

Betty Friedan publishes *The Feminine Mystique.*

1964

Title VII of the Civil Rights Act bars sex discrimination in employment in business with over twenty-five employees.

1966

The National Organization of Women is founded with Betty Friedan as its first president.

1967

Executive Order 11375 expands President Lyndon Johnson's affirmative action policy to cover sex discrimination. Federal agencies and contractors must try to ensure that women, as well as minorities, have the same opportunities as white males.

1968

Protesters demonstrate against the Miss America Pageant.

1969

Cornell University in Ithica, New York offers the first women's studies courses. President Richard Nixon signs an executive order requiring affirmative action in the federal government.

1971

In *Phillips v. Martin Marietta* the Court rules that businesses cannot refuse to hire women because they have small children unless they also refuse to hire men with small children. President Richard Nixon vetoes federally funded day care. *Ms.* magazine first appears as an insert in *New York* magazine. The Boston Women's Health Collective publishes *Our Bodies, Ourselves.* *Reed v. Reed* bars arbitrary preference for men in state laws. The Equal Employment Opportunity Commission files a 23,000 page report calling AT&T the "largest oppressor of women workers" in the United States.

1972

The Equal Rights Amendment, first proposed in 1972, passes Senate. The deadline for state ratification is set for 1979.

1973

Roe v. Wade abolishes state laws prohibiting abortion during the first three months of pregnancy on grounds that the laws interfere with a woman's right to private control of her body. Universities start establishing athletic scholarships for women. AT& T signs $38 million settlement with Equal Employment Opportunity Commission and Department of Labor. The AFL-CIO (the American Federation of Labor–Congress of Industrial Organizations) backs the Equal Rights Amendment; thirty states have ratified it. The first battered women shelters open in Minnesota and Boston. U.S. Tennis Association awards equal prize money to women in the U.S. open. Billy Jean King beats Bobby Riggs in straight sets in a match called "The Battle of the Sexes." The National Organization of Women demonstrates against the Little League World Series, which bars women. A New Jersey court calls the no-girls rule illegal.

1974

The Equal Credit Opportunity Act bars credit discrimination on basis of sex or marital status. The first women are ordained in the Episcopal Church. The Fair Housing Act of 1968 is extended to bar sex discrimination.

1975

Congress passes legislation opening military academies to women. Susan Brownmiller publishes *Against Our Will*, which re-defines rape as a crime of violence rather than of sexuality. The American Psychological Association takes homosexuality off its list of mental disorders.

1976

The Supreme Court rules that states cannot require a woman wanting an abortion to get consent from her husband or single girls under eighteen to get permission from a parent. Del Martin publishes *Battered Wives*, the first major report on domestic abuse. *Ms.* magazine counts ten shelters for battered women in the country. NASA starts training women to be astronauts.

1978

The Pregnancy Discrimination Bill bars firing, not hiring, or not promoting women because of pregnancy. Nancy Kasselbaum is elected to the Senate, becoming the first female senator who is not the widow of a congressman. The deadline for ratification of the Equal Rights Amendment is extended. The National Organization of Women organizes a boycott of states that haven't ratified. 100,000 march for the Equal Rights Amendment in Washington, D.C.

1979

Five states—Delaware, Iowa, Nebraska, New Jersey and Oregon—have laws allowing husbands who rape their wives to be prosecuted.

1980

According to the Women's Committee of the Director's Guild, of the 7,332 movies released by major American studios between 1949 and 1979, only fourteen were directed by women. The Democratic party decides on equal representation of men and women on all its committees.

1981

Sandra Day O'Connor becomes the first woman appointed to the Supreme Court. President Reagan backs the Human Life Amendment, a proposed constitutional amendment banning abortion and some forms of birth control.

1982

The Equal Rights Amendment falls three states short of ratification.

1983

Sally Ride becomes the first female astronaut in America. Christine Craft sues a television station for firing her because she was deemed "too unattractive, too old and not deferential enough to men."

1984

Geraldine Ferraro runs on Democratic ticket for vice-president.

1985

Marital rape is now a criminal offense in twenty-three states; fifteen states are considering similar laws.

1986

125,000 march in Washington to keep abortion and birth control legal, the largest women's rights gathering in history. In *Merritor Savings Bank v. Vinson* the Supreme Court rules that sexual harassment on the job is a form of gender discrimination and thus in violation of Title VII of the Civil Rights Act. H.W. Janson's *History of Art*, a standard college art history textbook, incorporates female artists for the first time in its third edition. The U.S. Supreme Court rules that an Indianapolis ordinance written by Catherine McKinnon and Andrea Dworkin, which had defined pornography as discrimination against women, is unconstitutional. Congress approves stricter federal rape laws. The single crime of rape is replaced with four gradations of severity, penalties are based on severity, and the exemption for marital rape is abolished.

1989

President George Bush vetoes a bill that would permit the use of Medicaid to fund abortions for poor women who are victims of "promptly reported" rape or incest.

1990

President George Bush signs legislation requiring the government to collect hate crime statistics based on race, ethnicity, religion and sexual orientation. Crimes motivated by gender are not included.

1991

The Supreme Court rules in *Automobile Workers v. Johnson Controls* that Title VII forbids sex-specific fetal-protection policies. Of the 540,000 troops active in the Gulf War, 35,000 are women.

1992

The American Association of University Women publishes a report titled "Shortchanging girls, shortchanging America," discussing gender discrimination in schools. A women's bathroom is installed in the Senate after a record-breaking number of women (six) are elected. The Senate Judiciary Committee reports that in the previous year there were about a million attacks on women by their husbands or lovers and another three million domestic assaults that were unreported. A report published by the National Collegiate Athletic Association says that for every woman playing Division I college sports, there are 2.24 men. Similarly, the report says that more than twice as many men as women receive athletic scholarships. Congress passes the Freedom of Access to Clinic Entrances Act, which makes it illegal to block, intimidate, or interfere with people visiting abortion and reproductive health clinics.

1995

NBC reports that there were 1,700 acts of violence against abortion providers between 1977 and 1994.

1996

In *United States v. Virginia et al.,* the Supreme Court rules that Virginia's categorical exclusion of women from Virginia Military Institute denies equal protection to women.

1997

California enacts Proposition 209, a state ban on all forms of affirmative action.

1998

The Supreme Court rules in *Faragher v. City of Boca Raton* that in some circumstances employers can be held responsible for sexual harassment by a supervisor.

1999

In *Davis v. Monroe Country Board of Education* the Supreme Court rules that a school board can be held responsible for student-on-student harassment in cases where the harassment is severe enough to deprive the victim of equal education opportunities and the school knows about the sexual harassment but does nothing about it.

2001

Nancy Pelosi is elected to the position of Minority Whip in the U.S. Congress, to date the highest position held by a woman.

FOR FURTHER RESEARCH

Books

Jennifer Baumgardner and Amy Richards, *Manifesta: Young Women, Feminism, and the Future.* New York: Farrar, Straus & Giroux, 2000.

Barbara J. Berg, *The Remembered Gate: Origins of American Feminism: the Woman and the City, 1800–1860.* New York: Oxford University Press, 1978.

Patricia Hill Collins, *Black Feminist Thought: Knowledge, Consciousness, and the Politics of Empowerment.* Boston: Unwin Hyman, 1990.

Nicholas Davidson, *The Failure of Feminism.* Buffalo, NY: Prometheus Books, 1988.

Susan Faludi, *Backlash: The Undeclared War Against American Women.* New York: Crown, 1991.

Barbara Findlen, ed., *Listen Up: Voices From the Next Feminist Generation.* Seattle: Seal Press, 1995.

Betty Friedan, *The Feminine Mystique.* New York: Dell Publishing Co., 1963.

Beverly Guy-Sheftall, *Words of Fire: An Anthology of African-American Feminist Thought.* New York: New Press: Distributed by W.W. Norton, 1995.

bell hooks, *Ain't I a Woman: Black Women and Feminism.* Boston: South End Press, 1981.

———, *Talking Back: Thinking Feminist, Thinking Black.* Boston: South End Press, 1989.

Patricia Ireland, *What Women Want.* New York: Dutton, 1996.

Linda S. Kauffman, *American Feminist Thought at Century's End: A Reader*. Cambridge, MA: Blackwell, 1993.

Michael S. Kimmel and Thomas E. Mosmiller, *Against the Tide: Pro-Feminist Men in the United States, 1776–1990: A Documentary History*. Boston: Beacon Press, 1992.

Laura Lederer, ed. *Take Back the Night: Women on Pornography*. New York: Morrow, 1980.

Jane J Mansbridge, *Why We Lost the USA*. Chicago: University of Chicago Press, 1986.

Keith E. Melder, *Beginnings of Sisterhood: The American Woman's Rights Movement, 1800–1850*. New York: Schocken Books, 1977.

John Stuart Mill, *The Subjection of Women*. New York: D. Appleton and Company, 1869.

Katie Roiphe, *The Morning After: Sex, Fear, and Feminism on Campuses*. Boston: Little, Brown and Co., 1993.

Anne Wilson Schaef, *Women's Reality: An Emerging Female System in a White Male Society*. San Francisco: Harper & Row, 1985.

Miriam Schneir, ed., *Feminism in Our Time: The Essential Writings, World War II to the Present*. New York: Vintage Books, 1994.

Barbara Smith, ed., *Home Girls: A Black Feminist Anthology*. New York: Kitchen Table—Women of Color Press, 1983.

Elizabeth Cady Stanton; Susan B. Anthony; Matilda Joslyn Gage, eds., *History of Woman Suffrage*. Salem, NH: Ayer, 1985.

Gloria Steinem, *Moving Beyond Words*. New York: Simon and Schuster, 1994.

Nadine Strossen, *Defending Pornography: Free Speech, Sex, and the Fight for Women's Rights*. New York: Scribner, 1995.

Rebecca Walker, ed. *To Be Real: Telling the Truth and Changing the Face of Feminism.* New York: Anchor Books, 1995.

Naomi Wolf, *Fire with Fire: The New Female Power and How It Will Change the 21st Century.* New York: Random House, 1993.

Mary Wollstonecraft, *A Vindication of the Rights of Woman.* New York: Cambridge University Press, 1995.

Virginia Woolf, *A Room of One's Own.* New York: Harcourt Brace Jovanovich, 1929.

Cathy Young, *Ceasefire!: Why Women and Men Must Join Forces to Achieve True Equality.* New York: Free Press, 1999.

Periodicals

Sharon Begley, "A Crucial Test for Feminism," *Newsweek*, October 30, 2000.

Patricia Cohen, "A Woman's Worth: 1857 Letter Echoes Still: Some Basic Disputes Over Feminism Still Persist," *New York Times*, July 18, 1998.

Economist. "Feminism Is Motherhood," The Economist Newspaper Ltd., March 13, 1999.

Jennifer Frey, "Feminism's Unblushing Bride: Gloria Steinem's Marriage Surprises Fellow Activists," *Washington Post*, September 7, 2000.

Ted Gest and Elisabeth Blaug, "The Women Win—Again," *U.S. News & World Report*, April 6, 1987.

Elizabeth Kastor, "A Date with Controversy," *Washington Post*, January 12, 1998.

Judy Klemesrud, "Americans Assess 15 Years of Feminism," *New York Times*, December 19, 1983.

Elizabeth Kolbert, "Literary Feminism Comes of Age," *New York Times*, December 6, 1987.

Jamie Malanowski, "Racists for Feminism! The Odd History of the Civil Rights Bill," *Washington Post*, February 6, 1994.

Jane Mansbridge and Barbara Smith, "How Did Feminism Get to Be All White?" *American Prospect*, March 13, 2000.

Marilyn Milloy, "The New Feminism," *Essence*, September 1997.

Ann O'Hanlon, "A Sense of Scale," *Washington Post Magazine*, January 5, 1997.

Eloise Salholz, et al., "Feminism's Identity Crisis," *Newsweek*, March 31, 1986.

Alvin P. Sanoff, "The Mixed Legacy of Women's Liberation," *U.S. News & World Report*, February 12, 1990.

Michele Wallace, "When Black Feminism Faces the Music, and the Music Is Rap," *New York Times*, July 29, 1990.

Marjorie Williams, "The Ms. Mystique: Feminism Puts On a Pretty Face," *Washington Post*, August 3, 1988.

Kenneth L. Woodward, et al., "Feminism and the Churches," *Newsweek*, February 13, 1989.

Cathy Young, "Equal Cultures—or Equality? There's a Choice to Be Made Between Feminism and Multiculturalism," *Washington Post*, March 29, 1992.

Tara Zahra, "The Feminism Gap," *American Prospect*, January/ February 1999.

INDEX